RICOEUR AND KANT
Philosophy of the Will

ÆR

American Academy of Religion
Studies in Religion

Editor
David E. Klemm

Number 66
RICOEUR AND KANT
Philosophy of the Will

by
Pamela Sue Anderson

RICOEUR AND KANT
Philosophy of the Will

by
Pamela Sue Anderson

Scholars Press
Atlanta, Georgia

RICOEUR AND KANT
Philosophy of the Will

by
Pamela Sue Anderson

© 1993
The American Academy of Religion

Library of Congress Cataloging in Publication Data
Anderson, Pamela Sue.
  Ricoeur and Kant: philosophy of the will/ by Pamela Anderson.
    p. cm. — (Studies in religion)
  Includes bibliographical references.
  ISBN 1–55540–836–2 (alk. paper). — ISBN 1–55540–837–0 (alk.
paper)
    1. Ricoeur, Paul. 2. Kant, Immanuel, 1724–1804—Influence.
3. Will.   I. Title.   II. Series: AAR studies in religion; no. 66.
B2430.R554A63 1993
128'.3—dc20   93–16101
                                             CIP

Printed in the United States of America
on acid-free paper

Contents

Preface

The reader may find that, at least in part, the text which follows is distanced from and critical of Paul Ricoeur. However, my goal has been and remains a critical, but sympathetic reconstruction of Ricoeur's project. Since 1980 when I first met Ricoeur during his Sarum Lectures at Oxford University, my work has exhibited a notable focus. Although unusual, my reading Ricoeur in the context of a British university for over ten years still gives a unique and, I believe, significant focus to my work. Many of my questions concerning transcendental idealism, in particular, reflect the influence of Anglo-American philosophers—but I do not strictly write with analytical philosophers in mind. I hope to make Ricoeur more accessible to contemporary theologians on both sides of the Atlantic, as well as to Anglo-American philosophers generally.

My title reflects a bold attempt to confront not only Ricoeur, but also the philosophical sage, Immanuel Kant. I do not presume to have achieved the heights of contemporary Kantian scholarship. However, I must acknowledge my debt to recent work on Kant by Onora O'Neill, Allen Wood and Henry Allison—their work has stretched my thinking in various ways. In this regard, I must give personal thanks to Alan Montefiore, Balliol College, Oxford for my initiation into seriously reading Kant. Montefiore has not edited what I have written in this book, but the very idea of my writing on Ricoeur and Kant would not have been possible without his teaching and his encouragement over the years.

To the world of theology, I must also acknowledge a debt. I thank John Macquarrie, Christ Church, Oxford who first supported my study of Ricoeur's early works. Also, at one crucial stage in my intellectual development David Brown, then Oriel College, Oxford helped with the difficult task of learning to simplify overly complex thoughts and sentences. Without Macquarrie and Brown, my struggle to articulate the timely theological significance of Ricoeur's philosophy of the will would have been very different.

Finally, I am grateful to the editor of the AAR Studies in Religion series, David E. Klemm. Klemm's consistent faith in the great value of my work on Ricoeur has made this book possible.

all hermeneutics are Kantian
to the degree that...
the limited character of self-knowledge
imposes an indirect strategy
of interpretation

Ricoeur 1971

Introduction

For many intellectuals Paul Ricoeur remains an enigma. Consistent with
Ricoeur's early Kantian assumptions concerning the inscrutable aspect of
every human subject, we might think that an enigma of personal identity
is inevitable. Yet if we also take seriously Ricoeur's later argument
concerning the possibility of narrative identity giving a meaningful unity
to the constantly changing subject of human experience, we would find
ourselves compelled to seek a coherent account of Ricoeur as the self-
same subject.[1] I critically interpret the early Ricoeur in order to offer
conditions for coherence with the later Ricoeur.

On first inspection of his identity over time it is difficult, if not
impossible, to pin down "Paul Ricoeur." We might again find this
difficulty consistent with Immanuel Kant's argument concerning
numerical identity; Kant counters the rationalist assumption that the self
is identical through time.[2] Contemporary twentieth-century French
philosopher, theologian, hermeneuticist, and critical theorist, Ricoeur
himself seems to exemplify the problem of the constantly changing
subject, continually speaking from and for different points of view. In
dialogue since 1935 with French and German traditions, and with Anglo-
Americans since at least 1945, Ricoeur has written on most major post-
war issues. Author of works on existentialism and phenomenology,
structuralism and psychoanalysis, metaphor and narrative, ethics and
religion, Ricoeur has endeavored to engage various twentieth-century

---

[1] Paul Ricoeur, *Time and Narrative*, III, trans. Kathleen Blamey and David Pellauer
(Chicago: University of Chicago Press, 1988), pp. 246–49; also see my "Narrative
Identity and the Mythico-Poetic Imagination," in David E. Klemm and William
Schweiker (eds), *Meanings in Texts and Actions: Questioning Paul Ricoeur*
(Charlottesville: The University Press of Virginia, 1993), pp. 195–204.
[2] See Kant's discussion of the paralogisms of pure reason in the transcendental
dialectic, *Critique of Pure Reason*, trans. Norman Kemp Smith (London: Macmillan
1950), A362–67 and B404 & B408–13. Cf. Ricoeur, "Narrative Identity," in David
Wood (ed.), *On Paul Ricoeur: Narrative and Interpretation* (London: Routledge, 1991),
pp. 188–200.

intellectuals. In the light of—even in spite of—what may seem ineluctably enigmatic, I want to argue that a significant and consistent reading of Ricoeur can be achieved by scrutinizing his early project in writing a philosophy of the will.

I intend to demonstrate that Ricoeur's seminal project on the will reveals a crucial debt to Kant; and I contend that a post-Kantian account of a dual-aspect subject remains at the core of all his thinking. This means that, according to Ricoeur's account of human willing, the subject is not merely passive in receiving the intuitions of experience but is actively involved in the constitution of objective experience and in the self-recognition of human freedom as a captive free will. We should see that this account of a dual-aspect subject as both active and passive, rational and sensible, provides a framework for critically interpreting Ricoeur's ongoing project. In line with Ricoeur's own self-description, his account will be identified as "post-Hegelian Kantian."[3] Not unlike other French intellectuals in the 1930s, Ricoeur does philosophy—even reconstructs Kant's account of the subject—in the wake of G.W.F. Hegel and German idealism.[4]

---

[3] Ricoeur, *The Conflict of Interpretations: Essays in Hermeneutics*, I, edited Don Ihde (Evanston: Northwestern University Press, 1974), pp. 412–16. See the next chapter section three, "A post-Hegelian Kantian standpoint."

[4] In *Modern French Philosophy*, trans. Linda Scott-Fox and J. M. Harding (Cambridge: Cambridge University Press, 1980), Vincent Descombes gives a historical account of Hegel's significant place in twentieth-century French thought. In particular Descombes recognizes the importance for French phenomenologists, structuralists, marxists, cultural and literary theorists of Alexandre Kojève's lectures on Hegel delivered at *L'Écoles Pratiques des Hautes Études* in Paris between 1933 and 1939. Notes and texts of Kojève's lectures are assembled by Raymond Queneau, who attends the lectures, and are published by Gallimard in 1947; these are published in an abridged version, Alan Bloom (ed.) *Introduction to the Reading of Hegel*, trans. J. H. Nichols (New York: Basic Books, 1969). Also important from the 1930s until 1968 is the influence of Jean Hyppolite who gave seminars on Hegel's *Phenomenology of Spirit* at *L'École Normale Supérieure and the Collège de France*. See *Phenomenology of Spirit*, trans. A. V. Miller (Oxford: Oxford University Press, 1977); and Hyppolite, *Genesis and Structure of Hegel's Phenomenology of Spirit*, trans. Samuel Cherniak and John Heckman (Evanston: Northwestern University Press, 1974). On the basis of the master/slave dialectic in Hegel's *Phenomenology of Spirit*, Kojève stresses that the struggle between mastery and slavery constitutes the major dynamic of history; this struggle links individual self-conscious subject and social-cultural development. Hyppolite, in contrast, emphasizes a characteristic striving, like that represented by Hegel's "unhappy consciousness," of the creative subject for stability in a chaotic world; the unhappy consciousness portrays subjectivity as always divided and longing for reconciliation. In chapter one I discuss Ricoeur's post-Hegelian Kantian standpoint. For further background on Kojève and Hyppolite, and also on Eric Weil

One important point to keep in mind is that what I call a fundamental post-Kantian account of the dual-aspect subject is not necessarily explicit in all Ricoeur's writings. For instance, there are places where Ricoeur obviously does not assume that Kant holds a dual-aspect account of experience; this appears to be the case with the later Ricoeur's critical discussions of Kantian formalism in Anglo-American ethical theory.[5] But I would still maintain that Ricoeur's criticism of "an overly formal Kant" is not inconsistent with either Kant or Ricoeur actually holding an account of a self-same rational and sensible subject.[6]

To return to what might be called his numerical identity, Paul Ricoeur was born on 27 February 1913 in Valence, France. Ricoeur lost both his parents by the time he was two years old; his father died fighting in World War I. He and his sister were brought up by an aunt. Ricoeur himself admits that his childhood experiences left him with a sense of conflict between reason and his emotions on questions such as war; and on a more general, intellectual level he continues to maintain a sharp separation between philosophy and religion. Ricoeur recognizes, in what we will find to be highly Kantian terms, that reason and his deepest emotions remain in tension, at times producing a definite sense of split identity.[7]

---

who studied under Kojève and whose post-Hegelian Kantianism influences Ricoeur, see Micheal S. Roth, *Knowing and History: Appropriations of Hegel in Twentieth-Century France* (Ithaca: Cornell University Press, 1988), especially pp. 3–5, 19–28, 37–39, 84, 94–103, 151–54, 176–86.

[5] Ricoeur, *Soi-même comme un autre* (Paris: Editions du seuil, 1990), pp. 239–76, 305–29; *Oneself as Another*, trans. Kathleen Blamey (Chicago: Chicago University Press, 1992), pp. 204–18, 262–83; and "Practical Reason," trans. Kathleen Blamey, in *From Text to Action: Essays in Hermeneutics*, II (Evanston: Northwestern University Press, 1991), pp. 198–200.

[6] For the development of this interpretation, with certain changes, in Ricoeur's later work see for example, *Soi-même comme un autre*, pp. 142, 144–45, 145n1, 146 & 150n1; *Oneself as Another*, pp. 118, 119n4, 120n5, 124n11, 125. Also see my "A Question of Personal Identity," *The Personalist Forum*, vol. VIII, no. 1 (spring 1992), pp. 55–68.

[7] In a recent interview with Charles Reagan, Ricoeur reflects upon these emotions and describes in French *une schizophrénie* created by the intensity of conflicts between his feelings for pacificism and his reasons for responsible action [e.g. against Hitler]; he similarly describes an inner conflict between religion and philosophy. See Charles Reagan, *"Interview avec Paul Ricoeur: le 8 juillet 1991," Bulletin de la Société américaine de philosophie de langue française*, vol. III, no. 3 (winter), pp. 158–68.

In 1935 Ricoeur marries Simone Lejas—this year equally marks the point at which the record of his significant publications begins.[8] Ricoeur's earliest published essays tend to focus on Christian socialism, pacificism, and truth in history.[9] His focus matures when, in the 1930s, Ricoeur studies philosophy at the Sorbonne in the intellectual context of French existentialism and phenomenology. His existentialist mentor, Gabriel Marcel, has a lasting influence on his thought, while Ricoeur's detailed study of phenomenology occurs as a result of being captured early in World War II. During his five years as a prisoner of war, 1940–45, he gains access to the works of Edmund Husserl as well as to those of the German philosophers Martin Heidegger and Karl Jaspers. Publishing his French translation of and authoritative commentary on Husserl's *Ideen, I* in 1950 initially establishes Ricoeur as an existential phenomenologist; this translation becomes the first in Jean-Paul Sartre's and Maurice Merleau-Ponty's *Bibliothèque de philosophie*. Also in 1950 Ricoeur completes the first volume in his philosophy of the will—to which I turn in the next chapter. There I intend to describe the *prima facie* opposing influences of Marcel and Husserl on Ricoeur before exposing the more fundamental post-Kantian presuppositions which hold together the diverse aspects of Ricoeur's project on the will. It is the post-Kantian development of his thought which eventually establishes Ricoeur as a hermeneutical phenomenologist.[10]

Only two out of three of Ricoeur's projected volumes on the will have been completed. *Philosophie de la volonté*, I. *Le volontaire et l'involontaire* was first published in 1950; *Philosophie de la volonté*, II. *Finitude et culpabilité*, 1. *L'homme faillible*; 2. *La symbolique du mal* in 1960. These are translated into English as three separate books: *Freedom and Nature: The Voluntary and the Involuntary* (1966), *Fallible Man* (1965) and *The Symbolism of Evil* (1967).[11] I base my argument largely upon these three books. However, I find support from his later works for my contention concerning Ricoeur's post-Kantian account of the subject. It is not possible in the present context to complete an adequate intellectual biography because this would have to include Ricoeur's publication of over 700 articles and 12 major works, besides his actual involvement with

---

[8] Frans D. Vansina, *Paul Ricoeur: A Primary and Secondary Systematic Bibliography (1935–84)* (Louvain-la-Neuve: Éditions de L'institut supérieur de philosophie, 1985).

[9] Charles Kelbley, "Translator's Introduction," in *History and Truth* (Evanston: Northwestern University Press, 1965), pp. xi–xxi.

[10] Ricoeur, "Phenomenology and Hermeneutics," *Nous* 9 (1975), pp. 85–102.

[11] See bibliography for details on each publication.

various contemporary issues. Yet what follows is mention of certain major works, along with brief statements of Ricoeur's ever-evolving itinerary.

During the same period as the appearance of his works on the will Ricoeur has two major collections of essays published. One collection is a compilation of writings entitled *History and Truth* (1964); the other is a collection translated as *Husserl: An Analysis of His Phenomenology* (1967). Then, while completing the second book of the second volume in his philosophy of the will, *The Symbolism of Evil*, Ricoeur becomes concerned with the challenges being addressed to phenomenological reflection by linguistics, psychoanalysis, and structuralism. His growing preoccupation with language and hermeneutics, as well as with debates concerning the decentered subject, culminates in his publishing a major work on *Freud and Philosophy: An Essay on Interpretation* (1970) and essays on *The Conflict of Interpretations: Essays in Hermeneutics* (1974). I use these two publications to emphasize the crucial importance of Ricoeur's confrontation with three masters of suspicion, i.e. Marx, Nietzsche, and Freud.

During these years in the '60s of intellectual challenge and transition, Ricoeur also finds himself at the center of the 1968 student struggle in Paris. Supporting reform of the French university Ricoeur is made dean, in 1968, of the new university campus at Nanterre just outside of Paris. At that moment he chooses to leave the Sorbonne and to support the students' cause. Yet very soon, in 1969 at a moment of extreme unrest, revolutionary students led by Daniel Cohn-Bendit turn against Ricoeur as figure of reform. Actual violence done to Ricoeur causes him to resign his position as dean and to rely upon his positions at the universities of Chicago and Louvain. Seen in retrospect leaving Nanterre to take up, with ever greater seriousness, his position at Chicago is opportune for Ricoeur's so-called split-identity—there he is able to maintain and explore the autonomy of reason in philosophy, on the one hand, and reason's relation to religion, on the other. Eventually his friendships with Hannah Arendt and Paul Tillich lead Ricoeur to gain the John Nuveen Chair in Philosophical Theology at the University of Chicago; this chair enables him to divide uniquely his time between philosophy and theology.

Along with changing employment comes Ricoeur's increased focus upon language and the creation of meaning. This focus is reflected in his *La métaphore vive* (1975). I make only passing reference to the translation, *The Rule of Metaphor: Multi-disciplinary Studies of the Creation of Meaning in*

Language (1978). However, I make more extensive use of passages from *Time and Narrative* I–III (1984–88), especially passages on time in Augustine, Kant, and Husserl. In this trilogy Ricoeur develops his previous work, on the creation of meaning in language, to present a theory of narrative that aims to unify the disparate aspects of temporal experience.

With *Time and Narrative*, III, we return to my opening statement that Ricoeur's later argument concerning narrative identity affords the possibility of giving a meaningful unity to the constantly changing subject of human experience. And Ricoeur is only able to conceive this unity by relying upon Kant's "synthesis of the heterogeneous."[12] In the chapters which follow I continue to elucidate Ricoeur's reliance on Kant in *Time and Narrative*.

At this point I feel bound to remark, however briefly, on Ricoeur's most recent work, *Oneself as Another* and "Self as *Ipse*."[13] *Oneself as Another* builds upon the fundamental Kantian argument that self-consciousness is not possible without an external world or "another." Essentially, in his *Critique of Pure Reason*, Kant demonstrates that the subject can only know itself as an object but to have even this limited knowledge it must be able, at the very same time, to distinguish itself from the object; the resulting, inevitably split subject knows itself inasmuch as it can recognize itself as an other. Or in Ricoeur's post-Kantian language, "self-same inasmuch as other." In "Self as *Ipse*" Ricoeur's reconstructs the subject as *ipse* (self-same) in order to avoid the atomistic pitfalls of both the so-called liberal self and the empiricist tradition; his conception of selfhood not only makes possible a discussion of human rights but, I would say, saves the post-Kantian self from the extreme formalism of Anglo-American ethical and political theory.

Before concluding this introduction I should explain the exegetical, restorative, and critical aims which underlie the present reconstruction of

---

[12] This reference is to Ricoeur's own formal description of the narrative's plot as presented in Kantian terms; cf. *Critique of Pure Reason*, B201–2. See Ricoeur, *Time and Narrative*, I, trans. Kathleen McLaughlin and David Pellauer (Chicago: University of Chicago Press, 1984), pp. 11, 65–66; *Time and Narrative*, III, p. 51; "Life in Quest of Narrative," in *On Paul Ricoeur*, pp. 21–24. See J. J. Lewis, "Synthesis and Category: the Synthesis of the Heterogeneous in Ricoeur and Kant," *Bulletin de la Société américaine de philosophie de langue française*, vol. III, no. 3, pp. 182–206.

[13] "Self as *Ipse*," the title of Ricoeur's yet unpublished 1992 Oxford Amnesty Lecture, is forthcoming in Basic Books; and *Oneself as Another* [*Soi-même comme un autre*], trans. Kathleen Blamey (Chicago: University of Chicago Press, 1992), first appeared just before publication of the present work.

Ricoeur's philosophy of the will. First, I endeavor to elucidate and bring together Ricoeur's variously significant ideas concerning human willing. This exegetical aim is important precisely because Ricoeur himself has not compiled in one work the enduring aspects of his own writings on the will; nor has he considered the implicit theological ideas that inform his project.

Second, I aim to demonstrate that Ricoeur's philosophy of the will contributes substantially to a restoration of a set of dualities: human freedom and nature, reason and desire, innocence and sin, non-time and time. For instance, an act of willing cannot be grasped phenomenologically without reconstructing both the voluntary moment of decision and the involuntary structures of our experience as temporal beings.[14] In other words Ricoeur aims to restore those dualities which have succumbed to critiques of modernity.[15] Two figures who represent modernity are Kant and Husserl; their critics include notably Marx, Nietzsche, and Freud, as well as certain French postmodern neo-Nietzscheans.

Third, I aim to consider critically Ricoeur's reading of Kant's philosophy. Ricoeur's reading assumes, as already mentioned, that the subject is not merely passive but is actively involved in the constitution of objective experience and in the self-recognition of human freedom. This account of the subject is *post*-Kantian insofar as it stays open to modification by Ricoeur's readings of subsequent modern figures, including Hegel, Marx, Nietzsche, and Freud. Moreover it is this enduring core account of a dual-aspect subject which, I contend, provides a framework for critically assessing the strengths and weaknesses of Ricoeur's hermeneutical phenomenology for modernity/postmodernity. I might add that I would include the feminist critique with the challenges posed for Ricoeur by postmodernity especially insofar as the rational subject is thought to be exclusively homogeneous and hopelessly male.[16]

---

[14] Ricoeur continues to develop this reconstruction of our experience as temporal beings; cf. *Soi-même comme un autre*, pp. 144–50; *Oneself as Another*, pp. 119–25.

[15] Ricoeur, *The Symbolism of Evil*, trans. Emerson Buchanan (New York/London: Harper and Row, 1967), pp. 349–56.

[16] See my "Hermeneutics of Tradition and the Decentered Subject," *Philosophy and Social Criticism* (forthcoming). For a timely work relating the modern philosophical "crisis," concerning subjectivity and rationality, to women and/in philosophy see Rosi Braidotti, *Patterns of Dissonance: A study in women in contemporary philosophy*, trans. Elizabeth Guild (Cambridge: Polity Press, 1991).

These implicit aims are reflected in three explicit claims. Exploring each of these claims in turn, in chapters one, two, and three, constitutes my detailed consideration of Ricoeur's contribution to contemporary philosophy and theology.

To begin with, I put forward the claim that the numerous contexts of the construction and the diverse forms of reception of Ricoeur's project call for the proposed Kantian reading of his philosophy of the will. Chapter one justifies this first claim to approach Ricoeur via Kant. It also supplies the critical ground for the intellectual legitimizing of Ricoeur's original project in its reading of the post-Kantian rational subject. I pose the question, How successful has Ricoeur been in both deconstructing the illusions of Kantian reason and reconstructing the unavoidable presuppositions of rational thought and action?

Next, in chapter two, I claim that Ricoeur contributes to the hermeneutical tasks of restoration and criticism. This claim is supported by Ricoeur's Kantian concepts of freedom, temporality/non-temporality and the mediating archetype of humankind, as well as by his post-Kantian critique of illusory ideas.

With Ricoeur I am, third, claiming that the dialectical relationship between the human and the divine is both constituted by and constitutive of the ontological and eschatological conditions of an implicit christology. In chapter three this christology is found to be paradigmatically represented by the myths of the first and second Adam. Implied is the view that any legitimation of Ricoeur's conceptions of freedom and grace depends not only upon the ontology but also upon the eschatology reflected in his hermeneutics of the symbolism of sin and salvation.

While offering a positive assessment of Ricoeur's symbolic account of freedom, I also argue that his dual-aspect account of human willing—privileging, as it does, the conceptual hypostases of the temporal and the non-temporal—is founded upon a transcendental idealist problematic. This being so, it becomes the legitimate target of a critique of ideology, of traditional morality, of religion and, in consequence and paradoxically, the object of Ricoeur's own "hermeneutics of suspicion."[17] Aware of this potentially delegitimating challenge to Ricoeur's Kantian reflections, my extended assessment of his symbolic account of the human and the divine nonetheless continues with the systematic reconstruction of his project. I believe that the critical and restorative aims which comprise his

---

[17] Ricoeur, *Freud and Philosophy: On Interpretation*, trans. Denis Savage (New Haven: Yale University Press, 1970), pp. 20–56.

project can be disentangled from the potentially mystifying nature of his dual-aspect account of the will.

The general claims of chapters one to three and the salvageable part of Ricoeur's critical restoration lead to a conclusion concerning the contribution which this study has endeavored to make towards going beyond Ricoeur's expressed project. I hope to move towards fundamental criticism of contemporary forms of knowledge and towards poetically constituted forms of transformative praxis. Of paramount importance in this regard, I will argue, is Ricoeur's projected poetics of human willing.

The book ends with a brief critical coda. This recapitulates the tensions inherent in Ricoeur's project between history as determining the limits on human willing and the horizon of eternity as constituting the transsignifying possibilities of the mythico-poetic imagination.[18]

---

[18] See my "Narrative Identity and the Mythico-Poetic Imagination," pp. 200–4.

1

Ricoeur's Kantian Project

My first general claim is that the numerous contexts of the construction and the diverse forms of reception of Ricoeur's project call for a Kantian reading of his philosophy of the will. I hope to justify this claim to approach Ricoeur via Kant and to legitimize intellectually Ricoeur's original project in its reading of the post-Kantian rational and sensible subject. To give further focus I will address the question as to how successful Ricoeur has been in both deconstructing the illusions of Kantian reason and reconstructing the unavoidable presuppositions of rational thought and action. In addressing this question I intend to shed new light on Ricoeur's project, as well as on his post-Kantian hermeneutics of "critical thought" and "restorative criticism."[1]

According to Kant critical thought is characterized by analysis and judgment, while critical judgment would make a decision concerning interpretations of its own thought.[2] According to Ricoeur,

> the hermeneutics of modern man[3] is continuous with the spontaneous
> interpretations that have never been lacking to symbols. ...what is peculiar
> to the modern hermeneutics is that it remains in the line of critical thought.
> ...we are in every way children of criticism, and we seek to go beyond

---

[1] Ricoeur, *The Symbolism of Evil*, p. 350.

[2] Immanuel Kant, *Critique of Pure Reason*, Axi–xiii, B142–43, A132–33/B171–72.

[3] In his translation of *The Symbolism of Evil*, Emerson Buchanan uses "man" as the English rendering of the French noun *l'homme*. Yet Ricoeur's use of *l'homme*, if consistent with its generic usage by other French phenomenologists, is assumed to mean human beings. Thus the preferred translation of other renderings of *l'homme* as "mankind" or "man" is "humankind" or "man or woman," respectively.

criticism by means of criticism, by a criticism that is no longer reductive but restorative.[4]

Ricoeur describes the interpretation of humankind's symbols as being spontaneous. Spontaneity is also a fundamental term in Kant's critical philosophy; spontaneity could easily be understood as the ungrounded ground of human reason. Thus understood Kantian spontaneity anticipates modern hermeneutics. It could even be argued that Kant's subordination of rationality to spontaneity has led to certain postmodern critiques of the modern project.[5]

Thomas McCarthy formulates the appropriate question for my legitimation of Ricoeur's reading of Kant:

> Are Kant's ideas of reason illusions of logocentric thinking that must tirelessly be deconstructed, or are they unavoidable presuppositions of rational thought and action that must carefully be reconstructed?[6]

The significant answer which I see Ricoeur providing involves a combination of a certain sort of deconstruction and reconstruction.[7] In terms more appropriate to Ricoeur we will find that his project is concerned with both post-Kantian critical thought and restorative criticism.

I. Contexts for a Philosophy of the Will

Ricoeur's project, beginning with the writing of *Le Volontaire et l'involontaire* and continuing on beyond *Finitude et culpabilité*, 1. *L'homme faillible*; 2. *La symbolique du mal*, aims at the construction of a philosophy of the will. Now this philosophy of the will confronts what Ricoeur himself describes as "an urgent task of contemporary thought" in

---

[4] Ricoeur, *The Symbolism of Evil*, p. 350.

[5] See Robert B. Pippin, *Modernism as a Philosophical Problem* (Oxford: Basil Blackwell, 1990) pp. 13–14, 51–61, 149–67. Cf. Kant, *Critique of Pure Reason*, B132, B150, B158n, B165, B430, B561–2; Ricoeur, *Time and Narrative*, III, p. 54ff; and *Soi-même comme un autre*, pp. 22, 126–29; *Oneself as Another*, pp. 11, 103–6.

[6] Thomas McCarthy, *Ideals and Illusions: On Reconstruction and Deconstruction in Contemporary Critical Theory* (Cambridge, MA: MIT Press, 1991), p. 1.

[7] Ricoeur does *not* follow Jacques Derrida in his use of deconstruction. For Ricoeur deconstruction is, roughly, the critical analysis of philosophical constructions and so something that might precede, or accompany, reconstruction; see footnotes 15 and 108 below. On deconstruction and Derrida see Christopher Norris, *Deconstruction: Theory and Practice*, rev edn (London: Routledge, 1991).

constructing an account of the human subject.[8] Ricoeur raises the question: what actually is it to give a comprehensive account of being human? His philosophy of the will reveals that, for him, a comprehensive philosophical anthropology is inevitably tied to theological reflection. I intend to demonstrate that Ricoeur's Kantian anthropology is intimately linked with his hermeneutics of the symbols and myths which point to the "losing hold of man[9] himself as belonging to the Sacred."[10]

Yet, if we ask about assessing Ricoeur's relation to modern and postmodern philosophy, to feminist anthropology, or to patriarchal theology, there exists a problem. From what standpoint can Ricoeur's project be accurately and fairly assessed for the contribution it is able to make to contemporary thought? Significant for us is that Ricoeur's philosophy of the will reconstructs certain—albeit controversial—aspects of the work of Kant. By stressing these aspects of Kant Ricoeur's writings provide us with a consistent[11] account of the human subject and a critical methodology. In fact Ricoeur's critical methodology develops from both Kant and hermeneutics.[12] Kant represents the critical thinker *par*

---

[8] Ricoeur, "The Antinomy of Human Reality and the Problem of Philosophical Anthropology," in Charles Reagan and David Stewart (eds), *The Philosophy of Paul Ricoeur: An Anthology of His Work* (Boston: Beacon Press, 1978), p. 20.

[9] For contemporary women Ricoeur's statement seems literally to refer to man. Perhaps because *l'homme*, when used in French phenomenology, has tended to serve as a generic reference for humankind Ricoeur remains unaware of the issue of gender in this context—a lack of awareness which is problematic in later contexts.

[10] *The Symbolism of Evil*, p. 37. Ricoeur defines myth, but not precisely, as a second-degree symbol which, by way of its narrative structure, elaborates the meaning of certain more fundamental primary symbols; ibid., pp. 5–8ff.

[11] By consistent I do not mean a fully coherent human subject, since Ricoeur's dual-aspect subject inevitably appears paradoxical; but consistent is used in the sense of the same account continuing to underlie Ricoeur's project.

[12] I do not give a very precise definition of hermeneutics. Ricoeur's works written since *The Symbolism of Evil* have addressed themselves to numerous aspects of hermeneutics; so a definition which is too specific would not do justice to these various works. I would, however, direct the reader to Ricoeur's "On Interpretation," which first appears in Alan Montefiore (ed.), *Philosophy in France Today* (Cambridge: Cambridge University Press, 1983), pp. 175–97; reprinted in *From Text to Action*, pp. 1–23. This essay presents Ricoeur's own reflection back upon the progression of his thought from his early neo-Kantian reflective philosophy (as defined by Jean Nabert) to his Husserlian phenomenology, to his "hermeneutical phenomenology" and, eventually, to his shift from interpreting written texts only to actions. A further point is that the development of Ricoeur's hermeneutics owes obvious debts to Martin Heidegger, Jürgen Habermas and, even more, to Hans-Georg Gadamer; cf. Ricoeur,

excellence, while Ricoeur's use of hermeneutics recognizes the need to decipher the signs of the human "effort and the desire to be" (*l'effort et le désir d'être*).[13] As he admits,

> I would say today that all hermeneutics are Kantian to the degree that the powerlessness of self-knowledge is the negative counterpart of the necessity to decipher signs given in me and outside me. It is the limited character of self-knowledge which imposes the indirect strategy of interpretation.[14]

I will attempt to demonstrate that Ricoeur's hermeneutics develops naturally from his Kantian analysis of human freedom and evil in his early volumes on the will. To offer only an outline of his philosophy of the will at this stage, Ricoeur's first volume, translated *Freedom and Nature: The Voluntary and the Involuntary*, constitutes an "eidetics" of the will. Here Ricoeur attempts a phenomenological analysis of the pure form of an act of willing. His second volume, translated *Finitude and Guilt* in two parts, *Fallible Man* and *The Symbolism of Evil*, constitutes an "empirics" and "mythics" of the will. His empirics describes the fallibility of human willing; the mythics interprets certain ancient symbols and narratives concerning the origin and end of evil. His subsequent reconstruction[15] in *Freud and Philosophy: On Interpretation*

Hermeneutics and the Human Sciences: Essays on language, action and interpretation, trans. and ed. John B. Thompson (Cambridge: Cambridge University Press, 1981). Yet I endeavor to push even these debts back to Ricoeur's fundamental debt to Kant and, specifically, to a post-Kantian account of the dual-aspect subject. This is *not* to say that I ignore Ricoeur's engagement with, for instance, Heidegger in order to avoid something which might decisively challenge my post-Kantian account. I do want to say that Ricoeur's thought changes and develops. But as in the case of "Heidegger and the Question of the Subject," Ricoeur does not find Heidegger's critique of the Cartesian (and by implication Kantian) subject absolutely decisive (*The Conflict of Interpretations*, pp. 223–35); for Ricoeur there remains "a positive hermeneutics of the 'I am' (p. 224)."

[13] Ricoeur acknowledges his debt to neo-Kantian, reflective philosopher Jean Nabert for this phrase in his preface to *Fallible Man*, trans. Charles Kelbley (Chicago: Henry Regnery, 1965), p. xxvi; cf. Jean Nabert, *Elements for an Ethic*, trans. William J. Petrek with a preface by Paul Ricoeur (Evanston: Northwestern University Press, 1969).

[14] Ricoeur, "Foreword," in Don Ihde, *Hermeneutic Phenomenology: The Philosophy of Paul Ricoeur* (Evanston: Northwestern University Press, 1971), p. xvi.

[15] Ricoeur uses reconstruction to describe his particular practice of philosophical interpretation; this is important for understanding his hermeneutical style of doing philosophy. He distinguishes his reconstruction from an "historical reading" which is content with seeking a certain degree of descriptive objectivity. In *Fallible Man* he claims that "the project of linking an empirics of the will to a mythics... had to be

deepens the debate concerning critical hermeneutics. As noted in my introduction, it is significant that in his reconstruction of Freud Ricoeur begins to confront the three masters of suspicion—Marx and Nietzsche as well as Freud. I contend that the critical methodology constituted by Ricoeur's dual hermeneutics of suspicion and faith becomes crucial to carrying out his original project.

The problem is, as suggested in the opening sentence of this chapter, Ricoeur's writings on the will are open to quite different—even conflicting—interpretations, but it is precisely this diversity which I believe calls for my *post*-Kantian reading. The several stages of Ricoeur's philosophy of the will alone—his eidetics, empirics, mythics, hermeneutics, and poetics of willing, as well as the different questions asked at each of these stages—provide the ground for various possible interpretations of his thought. In addition, his continuing involvement with intellectual issues means that a stand needs to be taken on what precisely constitutes his ongoing project.[16] For us, Kant's critical, dialectical thought serves as the model for preserving the tensions that characterize Ricoeur's project on the will—and for keeping it an open-

---

devoted to reconstruction" (p. xviii). Also Ricoeur claims not to "duplicate" but to "reconstruct," i.e. critically interpret, Freud's work in, "A Philosophical Interpretation of Freud," *The Conflict of Interpretations*, p. 162. I might add that the influence of Kant can be recognized in Ricoeur's manner of critically interpreting Freud; cf. my, *Paul Ricoeur's Philosophy of the Will* (unpublished DPhil thesis, Oxford University, 1989), chapter 5.

[16] It should be noted that Ricoeur's philosophy of the will remains incomplete. Certain publications from his mature writings might be put under the umbrella of his original project. J. M. Bernstein, in his review of the *Lectures on Ideology and Utopia*, suggests that Ricoeur's concepts of ideology and utopia could be placed under the proposed title of his originally projected third volume of "a poetics of the will... that is, an account of human beings as essentially creative beings" ["A Poetics of the Will," *The Times Higher Education Supplement* (27.3.87), p. 19]. In the editor's Introduction to the very same *Lectures*, George Taylor claims that "The breadth of Paul Ricoeur's work is unsurpassed by perhaps any other thinker in the world today" [*Lectures on Ideology and Utopia* (New York: Columbia University Press, 1985), p. i]. Notice that this comment is made before the completed translation of Ricoeur's *Time and Narrative*, I–III; and Ricoeur had not yet written the massive volume which grew out of his 1986 Gifford Lectures to which I refer in my introduction. Thus we confront the question of the most accurate and adequate approach to Ricoeur's ever-expanding project. In 1990 Stephen Clark asks the appropriate question, "on what major intellectual issues of the past forty years has Ricoeur not written with distinction" [*Paul Ricoeur* (London: Routledge, 1990), p. 2.] This question along with the preceding quotations, suggests that there could be definite objections to my claim that Ricoeur's project can be reasonably and accurately placed. Yet I remain firm in placing Ricoeur in a precise line with Kant.

ended project. Dialectical is introduced to describe this model of critical thought so that we allow for a characteristically *post*-Kantian development of Ricoeur's thought as defined by the identity of the subject in relation to an other.[17]

In order to defend my emphasis on Kant and to legitimize Ricoeur's account of the human subject, which moreover I maintain gives an underlying consistency and so coherence to his ongoing project, I will develop aspects of the intellectual biography began in my introduction. In particular in this chapter I want to give further context to the intellectual history in France as background to the content and method of Ricoeur's thought. The context is pertinent since the issues addressed in Ricoeur's philosophy of the will tend to emerge from contemporary debate; and his use of controversial aspects of Kant must be read along with other French readings of Kant and German phenomenology.

In 1933 when Ricoeur receives his *Licence ès Lettre*, from the University of Rennes, being philosophically orthodox means employing the tools of René Descartes and Immanuel Kant. Moreover Kant tends to be read in the light of Descartes, and not vice versa, insofar as French philosophers struggle with the problems associated with the Cartesian subject, the *ego cogito*.[18] But this orthodoxy is decisively challenged in the 1930s in France by the reception of German philosophers, G.W.F. Hegel, Edmund Husserl, and Martin Heidegger. The incredible impact of these three German "H's" upon orthodox French thought results in an attempted shift away from abstract idealism to supposedly concrete

---

[17] For discussion of this development in French thought see Vincent Descombes, *Le même et l'autre: Quarante cinq ans de philosophie française* (1933–78) (Paris: Les Editions du Minuit, 1979); trans. Linda Scott-Fox and J.M. Harding, *Modern French Philosophy* (Cambridge: Cambridge University Press, 1980). As Descombes explains, "'Subject' is the name given to a be-ing whose *identity* is sufficiently stable for it to bear, in every sense of the word (sustain, serve as a foundation for, withstand) change or modification. The subject remains the same, while accidental qualities are altered. Since Descartes, the most subjective of all subjects is the one which is certain of its identity, the ego of the *ego cogito*. The quality of subjectivity is thus confined to consciousness. But what is the dialectic, if not precisely a superior concept of identity ('speculative identity,' 'identity of identity and non-identity')" [p. 76; and see Montefiore's "Foreword," p. ix, also 13, 22–29, 75–76].

[18] Kerry H. Whiteside, *Merleau-Ponty and the Foundation of an Existential Politics* (New York: Princeton University Press, 1988), pp. 14–30 on Descartes, Kant and philosophical transition. Although Whiteside describes the philosophical foundations of Maurice Merleau-Ponty's politics, he gives some valuable historical information about philosophical orthodoxy and change in Paris at the time when Ricoeur writes the early volumes of his philosophy of the will.

philosophy—philosophy which has as its central problematic the subject and the other.[19] Maurice Merleau-Ponty, Jean-Paul Sartre, and Gabriel Marcel—Ricoeur's existentialist mentor at the Sorbonne—are all key figures in the French shift away from abstract to concrete questions about history and the meaning of human existence. By 1946 evidence of this shift is clear in Merleau-Ponty's confident assertion that

> All the great philosophical ideas of the past century—the philosophies of Marx and Nietzsche, phenomenology, German existentialism and psycho-analysis—had their beginnings in Hegel; it was he who started the attempt to explore the irrational and integrate it into an expanded reason, which remains the task of our century.[20]

Between 1933 and 1968 Hegel, although soon interpreted in the light of Husserl and Heidegger, does become the pivotal figure for French philosophy.[21] During this period of domination by German phenomenology, Hegel in particular provides a means for the French to try to understand the irrational—the violence—in history, as well as to understand the rational subject's relation to the other. However, by 1968 Gilles Deleuze and Michel Foucault reverse completely the value in which Hegel is held.[22] To achieve an adequate account of Ricoeur's work during these years of intellectual transitions, we must recognize the impact upon his early thought of the orthodox philosophers, Descartes and Kant, and their critics, Hegel, Husserl, and Heidegger from the

---

[19] Descombes, *Modern French Philosophy*, pp. 3–9, 16, 22–23, 108–9.

[20] Maurice Merleau-Ponty, *Sense and Non-sense*, trans. Hubert and Patricia Dreyfus (Evanston: Northwestern University Press, 1964), pp. 109–10; as the significant female contemporary of Sartre and Merleau-Ponty, Simone de Beauvoir also witnesses this shift to Hegel and to questions of meaning see de Beauvoir's *Force of Circumstance* trans. Richard Howard (New York: Putnam, 1965), p. 34.

[21] Michael Roth, *Knowing and History*, pp. 7n, 9, 60–69, 85, 89–92, 102–3.

[22] Descombes stresses that "In 1945, then, all that was modern sprang from Hegel and the only way to reconcile the contradictory demands of modernity was to advance an interpretation of Hegel. In 1968, all that was modern—that is, Marx, Freud, etc as before—was hostile to Hegel. The difference separating the two generations lies in the inversion of the sign that marked the relationship to Hegel: everywhere a *minus* was substituted for the plus. [Only] the reference point itself remained the same" (*Modern French Philosophy*, p. 12). For the assertion of an "anti-dialectical thinker" see Gilles Deleuze, *Nietzsche et la philosophie* (Paris: Presses Universitaire de France, 1962), p. 223; trans. Hugh Tomlinson, *Nietzsche and Philosophy* (London: Athlone, 1983), p. 195; and Michel Foucault, *L'ordre du discours* (Paris: Gallimard, 1971), p. 74.

1930s, as well as the critics of the three H's, Marx, Nietzsche, and Freud from at least 1968.

In my introduction we saw that Ricoeur's earliest published essays focus upon issues of history, truth, and violence (or pacificism). These issues are overdetermined by the contexts of Hegelian, existentialist, and Marxist debates in Paris between 1933 and 1968. Yet I contend that Ricoeur's first essays reflect a definite grounding in Cartesian/Kantian orthodoxy, at the same time as this background is modified somewhat by Ricoeur's engagement with Hegel and later the post-Hegelian critics. This contention is supported by Ricoeur's own self-description of being "post-Hegelian Kantian"—a self-description which he restates at various points in his continuing intellectual development.[23] But what does it mean to have a definite grounding in Cartesian/Kantian orthodoxy?[24]

Essentially I mean that Ricoeur remains concerned with the identity of the rational and sensible subject. Even today he is preoccupied with the history of the self-same subject, with personal and social identity despite change over time. In his earliest publications Ricoeur attempts to preserve both the subject and object of history.[25] In 1957 Ricoeur writes one particular review article, which may simply be fortuitous, yet whatever the case it is definitely revealing of his roots in post-Hegelian Kantianism. This review of Eric Weil's *Philosophie politique* (1956) appears in the journal, *Esprit*, edited by Emmanuel Mounier, who is the chief proponent of French personalism in Paris from 1932 until 1950, and with whom Marcel, Ricoeur, and Merleau-Ponty had involvement.[26] The value of Ricoeur's review for us lies in the fact that what he says reveals important affinities between Weil's post-Hegelian Kantian discussions of history, narrative, and identity and Ricoeur's early work on history and the subject, as well as his mature work on historiography and narrative identity.[27] Like Weil, Ricoeur begins with a Kantian grounding, next he

---

[23] See Ricoeur, *The Conflict of Interpretations*, p. 412; *Time and Narrative*, III, pp. 215, 226, 323 and 329; and *From Text to Action: Essays on Hermeneutics*, II, trans. Kathleen Blamey and John B. Thompson (Evanston: Northwestern University Press, 1991), pp. 197–202, 220–22.

[24] Montefiore, "Foreword," in *Modern French Philosophy*, pp. viii–ix; Whiteside, *Merleau-Ponty and the Foundation of an Existential Politics*, pp. 14–30; and Roth, *Knowing and History*, pp. 19–60.

[25] In particular Ricoeur, "Objectivity and Subjectivity in History," *Truth and History*, pp. 21–40.

[26] See my "A Question of Personal Identity," pp. 55–68.

[27] Ricoeur, "*La philosophie politique d'Eric Weil*," *Esprit* 25, no. 10 (October 1957), pp. 412–28; also his more recent, *Time and Narrative*, I, pp. 91–94, 121–74; III, pp. 193–206,

confronts the challenges posed by Hegel—as well as by Husserl, Heidegger, and those who follow—but then he claims to return to Kant's philosophy; in this regard they both use the self-description of post-Hegelian Kantian. But the question is whether or not they really "return": do they in fact ever turn against—give up—their Kantian *grounding* in the subject? The matter is not obviously straightforward, especially when, as Ricoeur admits, hermeneutics can even be viewed as Kantian. Here it should, at the very least, be kept in mind that Ricoeur's post-Hegelian reading of Kant is clearly informed by Weil's view that "*Il apparaît que le fondement dernier de la philosophie Kantienne doît être cherché dans sa théorie de l'homme, dans l'anthropologie philosophique*" (it appears that the ultimate foundation of Kantian philosophy must be sought in Kant's theory of man, in his philosophical anthropology).[28] Similarly, it appears that the ultimate foundation of Ricoeur's philosophy of the will must be sought in his Kantian account of the human subject—this is true despite his various debts to and constantly changing associations with contemporary existential, phenomenological, hermeneutical, and analytical philosophies.

The crucial point to be gleaned from the above is that the particular French reception of the three German H's, along with the orthodox French reading of Descartes and Kant, forces us to place Ricoeur in intellectual contexts with influential philosophical figures of his time in order to understand his Kantianism. In this case I see Weil as a mediating figure for Ricoeur. Weil attends Alexandre Kojève's seminal lectures on Hegel in Paris from 1934–38; Weil, who remains a self-confessed Kantian, could easily mediate, for Ricoeur, Kojève's influential reading of Hegel. I want to emphasize Ricoeur's characteristic sensitivity to his intellectual context and his constant involvement in contemporary political and cultural debates; this sensitivity and this involvement are distinctive marks of the twentieth-century Continental style of doing philosophy.[29]

208–16, 246–49. And I could make similar comments about Ricoeur to those made about Eric Weil's relations to Kant and Hegel by Roth, *Knowing and History*, pp. 151–55ff, 176–83. Cf. Eric Weil, "*De l'intérêt que l'on prend à l'histoire*," *Recherches philosophiques* 4 (1935); *Philosophie morale* (Paris: Vrin, 1961).

[28] Eric Weil, *Problèmes kantiens* (Paris: Vrin, 1963), p. 33.

[29] This Continental style might be contrasted with the Anglo-American style of doing philosophy which is virtually unconcerned with context; analytical philosophers are preoccupied with timeless arguments. Cf. Alan Montefiore (ed.), "Introduction," *Philosophy in France Today*; and Montefiore, "In and Out of Time," *The Times Literary Supplement* (17 January 1986), p. 68.

II. Reception of Ricoeur's Project

Let us move somewhat from contexts of construction to forms of reception of Ricoeur. No matter the diverse forms of the reception of his philosophy of the will, as represented by very different studies of his project, most readers have to take cognizance, at least to some degree, of Ricoeur's reading of Kant. We should consider some notable examples of this reception; but before anything else it should be unequivocally stated that *Fallible Man* remains without a doubt Ricoeur's most overtly Kantian book. In 1986 Ricoeur himself admits that this book is the one he favors the most of all his works; it is appropriate that in the same year *Fallible Man* is republished in a slightly revised version translated by Charles Kelbley.[30]

Numerous scholars have taken *Fallible Man* as the key to understanding Ricoeur. Ad Peperzak, in the introduction to his Dutch translation of certain essays from *The Conflict of Interpretations*, describes *Fallible Man* as Kant rethought and as Ricoeur's most underestimated work.[31] Also Michel Philibert rather exuberantly declares *Fallible Man* Ricoeur's most perfect work representing, as it does, his process of rethinking Kant.[32] Don Ihde characterizes *Fallible Man* as phenomenology within Kantian limits.[33] T. M. Van Leeuwen agrees with the view that references to Ricoeur's act of rethinking Kant should be understood in the light of Eric Weil; according to Van Leeuwen, *Fallible Man* reflects "the 'rethinking' of the philosophical anthropology which is…the real basis of Kant's thought."[34]

In the light of these remarks I would stress that my interpretation of Ricoeur depends to a large degree upon *Fallible Man*. In this work his Kantian philosophical anthropology is given a definite form. However, I have not taken this to be the sole basis of Ricoeur's Kantianism since *Freedom and Nature* had already begun his rethinking of Kant. A broadly

---

[30] Ricoeur, *Fallible Man*, revised trans. Charles Kelbley with an Introduction by Walter J. Lowe (New York: Fordham University Press, 1986); my page references are always to the 1965 translation unless otherwise stated.

[31] Ad Peperzak, *Inleiding* in *Wegan van de filosofie: Structuralism, psychoanalyse, hermeneutiek* (1970).

[32] Michel Philibert, *Paul Ricoeur ou la liberté de l'espérance*, Philosophes de tous les temps (Paris: Seghers, 1971).

[33] Don Ihde, *Hermeneutic Phenomenology*.

[34] T. M. Van Leeuwen, *The Surplus of Meaning: Ontology and Eschatology in the Philosophy of Paul Ricoeur* (Amsterdam: Rodopi, 1981), p. 44.

based interpretative context for reception of his post-Kantian thought finds support from several other studies.

To begin with, R. L. Hart claims that his ontology, in this case Ricoeur's fundamental ontology in *Freedom and Nature*, necessarily precedes his philosophical anthropology in *Fallible Man*.[35] Next, Walter Lowe appropriately argues that *Fallible Man* must be *penetrated* in order to proceed on an informed basis to interpret the rest of Ricoeur's voluminous writings.[36] Finally, it should be stressed that, as Patrick Bourgeois accurately demonstrates, Ricoeur's *Freedom and Nature* not only takes up Kant's question concerning the relation between natural causality and the transcendental causality of human freedom but in fact extends Kant's use of regulative ideas in order to understand human freedom.[37] Equally in his extension of Kant's ideas, Ricoeur develops his own emphasis upon the term limit to construct what F. D. Vansina already in 1963 identified as the foundation of Ricoeur's "reflective philosophy of limits."[38]

Not all reception of Ricoeur's early work has been positive. Noteworthy is that the English philosopher Mary Warnock in her 1967 review of *Freedom and Nature* is especially bothered by "a kind of theological assumption, or explanatory device, rather like the Fall," which she says,

> is at least one unexamined assumption in Ricoeur's book which may worry the scrupulous. We are told that there is, in man's relation with the universe, a phenomenon called the Fault, which just exists and which consists in a radical disruption of the world. By reference to this Fault various other phenomena, notably man's awareness of evil, are to be explained. But there is, at least in the present volume, virtually no discussion of the Fault itself.[39]

---

[35] R. L. Hart, *Unfinished Man and the Imagination: Toward an Ontology and a Rhetoric of Revelation* (New York: Herder and Herder, 1968).

[36] Walter Lowe, *Mystery of the Unconscious: A Study in the Thought of Paul Ricoeur* (New Jersey: Scarecrow Press, 1977).

[37] Patrick Bourgeois, *The Extension of Ricoeur's Hermeneutic* (The Hague: Martinus Nijhoff, 1975), pp. 11, 21–22, 31f.

[38] This 1963 article, from the Dutch journal *Tijdschrift voor filosofie*, by F. D. Vansina is translated into French as "*Esquisse, orientation et signification de l'entreprise philosophique de Paul Ricoeur (I–II)*," *Revue de métaphysique et de morale* 69 (1964) no. 2, pp. 179–208; no. 3, pp. 305–21.

[39] Mary Warnock, Book Review, *Philosophical Quarterly* (1967), p. 279; cf. Ricoeur, *Freedom and Nature: The Voluntary and the Involuntary*, trans. Erazim Kohak (Evanston: Northwestern University Press, 1966).

Ricoeur's assumption concerning the fall and his description of a phenomenon called the fault are further clarified in *Fallible Man* (1965). (Note that this book was published in English translation before *Freedom and Nature* and so should have been accessible to Warnock when she wrote her review of the first volume).

Yet I maintain that the explanatory devices which Ricoeur employs to introduce the inscrutable nature of evil and the myths concerning the origin and the end of evil are better understood in terms of those aspects of Kant's philosophy which bring together the dual viewpoints of the temporal and the non-temporal. It is precisely by clarifying Ricoeur's unargued assumptions that the critical interpretation of his philosophy of the will, which I am offering contributes to an understanding of his Kantian account of human willing. In particular Ricoeur uses such Kantian notions as radical evil in order to uncover certain of the deeply problematic issues of contemporary thought; and, as will be seen, this means criticizing the concept of original sin in order to restore meaning to narrative accounts of the mystery of evil.

It would be impossible for me to attempt to clarify all the apparent obscurities in Ricoeur's early work which were detected by analytical philosophers such as Mary Warnock. Warnock's largely negative appraisal of *Freedom and Nature* was part of a more general criticism of the philosophical style of twentieth-century France. She claimed that

> there is no doubt that the philosophical style of the twentieth century in France is one of the most barbarous styles there has ever been. Obscurity is piled upon obscurity, and the resulting language is an intolerable mixture of French and German.[40]

Warnock then concludes, concerning Ricoeur in particular and this French style of philosophy in general, that

> the practice of philosophy [is made] too easy, by removing the greatest difficulty there is in it, namely the absolute obligation of the philosopher to know exactly what he means.[41]

Such an analytical practice of assessing whether or not the philosopher has fulfilled this "absolute obligation...to know exactly what he means" is not my goal. Even if this practice was agreed to be possible, Ricoeur's philosophy of the will could not be fairly assessed according to

---

[40] Ibid.
[41] Ibid., p. 280.

this limited criterion. Instead my interpretation endeavors to identify the fundamental sources of the obscurities—or, as preferred here, the ambiguities—which can be discerned in Ricoeur's philosophical writings on the will. This is to say that these ambiguities have deeper reasons for their existence than either a lack of logical rigor or the inadequate development of an idea. Apparent ambiguities concerning Ricoeur's conceptions of human freedom, temporality, and non-temporality cannot merely be set right by the systematic clarification of his arguments appertaining to the will. The conflicting interpretations which appear in his work, as well as in its reception—and which are indeed recognized by Ricoeur himself—derive from the difficulties which inevitably attended the very complex project Ricoeur originally set himself in the development of a philosophy of the will.

Three main difficulties can be identified as having beset the reception of that original project. First, the scope of Ricoeur's project is enormous. His aim to move from a pure phenomenological analysis of the act of willing—his eidetics of willing—to an empirics of human fallibility, to a mythics or hermeneutics of the evil will, and finally to a poetics of the will has no definite point of completion; his poetics, and so his project, remains open-ended and ever-expanding. Second, Ricoeur's project incorporates different contrasted points of view as already noted at various points in the preceding. The views include Husserlian phenomenology, Kantian transcendental idealism, the lineage of German hermeneutics from Friedrich Schleiermacher to Wilhelm Dilthey, Martin Heidegger, Rudolf Bultmann, and Hans-Georg Gadamer, as well as modern Judaeo-Christian theology as it has been influenced especially by the idealist philosophy of G.W.F. Hegel and the dogmatic theology of Karl Barth. Third, Ricoeur set out to construct a philosophy of the will which would be rationally coherent, but which would also be deeply critical. He speaks of "destroying" as well as "restoring" what is assumed to be the meaning of human experience. Crucially, we will see that Ricoeur seeks to do away with certain theological assumptions concerning the concept of original sin while, at the very same time, he endeavored to restore meaning to the experience about which the penitent makes his or her confession.

The above said, I do not find Ricoeur's project in constructing a philosophy of the will to be incomplete—in the sense of a project left unfinished and abandoned—as William C. Placher contends.[42] Moreover, neither, as Placher might also lead one to suppose, is Ricoeur's early corpus of writings on the will—namely *Freedom and Nature, Fallible Man* and *The Symbolism of Evil*—patently contradictory; nor is this corpus unrelated to his essays on the will compiled in anthologies and other selected later writings.

Ricoeur's philosophy of the will is distributed amongst an ensemble of his writings devoted to issues which may be considered separately, but which are still essentially related concerns such as the possibility of evil and the actuality of "the fault."[43] Far from standing in a wholly disparate relation to each other the critical discourses centered on these separate issues gradually develop into unified stages of philosophical concern each in their own right; at the same time, they come together to constitute different levels of Ricoeur's philosophy of the will.

Consistent with his characteristic willingness to confront contemporary challenges to his own Cartesian and Kantian background, Ricoeur dedicates *Freedom and Nature*, his first volume in the philosophy of the will, to the French Roman Catholic philosopher, Gabriel Marcel. Marcel's concrete philosophy is thought to achieve a critical advance on both Descartes and Kant. As indicated in my introduction, Marcel is working in Paris when Ricoeur registers at the Sorbonne as a graduate student in the late 1930s. Ricoeur is ever indebted to Marcel for his notions of *le corps propre* and of the incarnate subject—notions which are also taken up by another of Ricoeur's contemporaries in French existential phenomenology, Maurice Merleau-Ponty.[44] Basically Marcel objects to the Cartesian reading of the body. Instead of being, in Descartes' sense, the source of uncertainty *les corps propres* (our own bodies) are our means of access to all that exists and as such the very

---

[42] William C. Placher, "Paul Ricoeur and Postliberal Theology: A Conflict of Interpretations?" *Modern Theology*, vol. 4, no. 1 (October 1987), p. 40.

[43] Ricoeur identifies the possibility of evil with fallibility and its actuality with "the fault," i.e. *la faille existentielle*; cf. *L'homme faillible* (Paris: Aubier, 1960), p. 92; *Fallible Man* (1965), pp. xxxvn, 114. In his introduction to the 1986 edition of *Fallible Man*, Walter J. Lowe emphasizes the importance of the terms which Ricoeur uses to describe "the fault," including *la faille, la faute, le déchirement, la fêlure* and *l'écart* (p. xxiii; except here my references follow page numbers in the 1965 edition).

[44] Ricoeur, *Gabriel Marcel et Karl Jaspers: philosophie du mystère et philosophie du paradoxe* (Paris: Éditions du temps présent, 1947); and *"Hommage à Merleau-Ponty,"* *Esprit* 29 (June 1961), pp. 1115–1120. For Ricoeur's continuing debt to Marcel and Merleau-Ponty see *Soi-même comme un autre*, pp. 369–80; *Oneself as Another*, pp. 319–29; and "Initiative," in *From Text to Action*, pp. 215–17.

condition of our ability to have knowledge of the world. Incarnation, or the incarnate subject, is the central given of metaphysics in that the subject is always embodied.[45] According to Marcel, the Cartesian epistemological and metaphysical rift between the uncertainty of the body and the certainty of the *cogito*, as well as a parallel rift between the world (or "other minds") and *ego cogito* (or "the subject"), need never have been opened. Both Ricoeur and Merleau-Ponty are profoundly influenced by Marcel's assertion that others are not, in the Cartesian sense, first alien to me and then accepted after a process of conscious reflection; I am from the start familiar with and open to others. Neither is my own body an alien object. In brief, to recognize *le corps propre* is to accept a theory of the mind that makes the idea of community comprehensible.[46]

Also important is that Marcel's influence directs Ricoeur to the formulation of a fundamental ontology characterized by questions of freedom, finitude, and hope—questions which, as we will find, connect nicely with Kant's practical writings. In addition in 1934, when he reads Marcel's *Journal métaphysique*, Ricoeur also carries out his first systematic reading of Edmund Husserl's *Ideen*, I. Ricoeur translates the Husserl work as part of the requirement for his *Doctorate d'état*, and both of these works, of Marcel and of Husserl, inform the writing of *Freedom and Nature* which is the thesis that fulfills the other part of the requirement for his doctorate.

The interplay between Marcel and Husserl in Ricoeur points to a fundamental characteristic of his critical methodology. As Ricoeur claims,

> Under the influence of Heidegger, Gabriel Marcel and Gadamer I have never ceased to distance myself from [Husserl's] subjective idealism.[47]

He further contends that subjective idealism is the "maleficent side" of phenomenology; and that, if Marcel's ontology of the other is

---

[45] Marcel, *Being and Having*, trans. K. Farrer (New York: Harper, 1965), pp. 11–12, 84–87.

[46] Merleau-Ponty, Review of *Etre et Avoir* by Gabriel Marcel *La Vie intellectuelle* 8:55 (10 October 1936), pp. 98–109; Ricoeur, *Soi-même comme un autre*, pp. 310–12; and "*Entre ethique et ontologie, disponibilité*," *Actes du Colloque Gabriel Marcel* (Paris: Bibliothèque nationale, 1989).

[47] Ricoeur, "Hegel and Husserl on Intersubjectivity," in *From Text to Action*, p. 234. Cf. Ricoeur's dialogue with Marcel in *Gabriel Marcel et la phénoménologie* (Neuchâtel: Les Éditions de la Baçonnière, 1973).

maintained, this maleficence can be avoided. Alternatively Ricoeur uses the hermeneutics of Martin Heidegger and Hans-Georg Gadamer to radicalize the aim of Husserl's reduction so that an encompassing relation of belonging unifies "the allegedly autonomous subject and the allegedly adverse object"; this relation is, according to Ricoeur's hermeneutic phenomenology, *prior* to the separation created by questions of objectivity.[48] The dialectical interplay between what might be perceived as conflicting aspects of Marcel and Husserl, or of concrete ontology and subjective idealism, becomes a crucial characteristic of the critical methodology which, as I claimed at the outset of this chapter, Ricoeur develops in his particular post-Kantian manner. And this interplay is not simply a uniting of differences—we will see again and again that Ricoeur warns against premature syntheses, against a Hegelian temptation.[49] Ricoeur does not use Kant (or Hegel), in any naive idealist sense, to unite opposing points of view; granted we may find that another form of idealism continues to haunt Ricoeur's project. Yet I attempt to demonstrate that the true art of Ricoeur's critical method lies in an aim to mediate by discovering unrecognized connections, while preserving differencess—even conflicts.

More specifically, in *Freedom and Nature*, Ricoeur creates an interplay between Marcel's incarnation of the subject and Husserl's reduction of the natural world. Husserl brackets-off the natural world according to an eidetic reduction, which constitutes a particular moment of phenomenological description. In theory the eidetic reduction holds in suspension all ontological assumptions and empirical meanings in order to make manifest the indubitable *eidos*—the intuited form—as the meaning of all human experience. The danger with the eidetic reduction, if actually possible, remains subjective idealism, as already suggested. To avoid this danger Ricoeur seeks to reconstruct Husserl's notion of intersubjectivity in a way which does not place the entire universe of meaning in a pure transcendental subject. Ricoeur recognizes that at best the aim of Husserl's reduction involves a paradox:

> The paradox is that it is only through this loss [of the natural world] that the world is revealed as "pregiven"; the body as "existing," and nature as "being" (*étant*). So the reduction does not take place between me and the

---

[48] Ricoeur, "Phenomenology and Hermeneutics," *Nous* (1975); reprinted in *From Text to Action*, p. 30.

[49] Ricoeur, "Preface to the First Edition (1955)," *History and Truth*, pp. 11–12; *Time and Narrative*, III, pp. 202ff.

world, between the soul and the body, between spirit and nature, but through the pregiven, the existing, and the being, which cease to be self-evident and to be assumed in the blind and opaque *Seinsglaube* (belief in being), becoming instead *meaning*: *meaning* of the pregiven, *meaning* of the existing, *meaning* of the being.[50]

The acceptance of this paradox—as the path to intersubjective meaning, not to solipsism—must be assumed by Ricoeur's phenomenological description of the meaning of willing. That is, in *Freedom and Nature*, Ricoeur assumes that human willing receives its deepest motives from the experience of some pre-given order of being. He also describes the experience of a pre-given order of being as "an absolute positing of a presence which constantly precedes my own power of self-affirmation."[51] For Marcel, the deepest mystery of human existence is that of being itself; incarnation reflects this mystery of the human being as a unity of body and soul. Concerning a mysterious pre-given order of being, I must admit the impossibility, in this context, of critically assessing whether or not Ricoeur succeeds in demonstrating Husserl's connection with Marcel. My concern is to re-emphasize that the very issue of a proper account of the human subject—whether a unified, split, or solipsistic subject—highlights the Kantian problematic at the center of Ricoeur's work.

Certainly Marcel's mystery of being can help us to understand Ricoeur's references to the transcendence which precedes the brokenness of our experiences of human willing.[52] Yet his other references to "Transcendence"[53] recall Ricoeur's polemical debate with Karl Jaspers concerning the ultimate ground of human existence. For Ricoeur, transcendence is experienced as the possibility and hope of a restoration of life's original innocence.[54] In contrast, for Jaspers, transcendence is experienced as an obscure ground of the self hidden in the depth of life's failures. According to Jaspers' account, human existence is, then, not structured by an original innocence but rather by a profound guilt.[55] In

---

50 Riceour, "Phenomenology and Hermeneutics," p. 28.
51 Ricoeur, *Freedom and Nature*, pp. 32–33.
52 Gabriel Marcel, *The Mystery of Being*, trans. G. S. Fraser (Chicago: Regnery, 1960).
53 Following Jaspers Ricoeur, in *Freedom and Nature*, refers to "Transcendence" with a capital "T"; cf. Ricoeur, *Gabriel Marcel et Karl Jaspers*, pp. 256ff.
54 Ricoeur, *Freedom and Nature*, pp. 26, 28–34.
55 Ricoeur, "The Relation of Jaspers' Philosophy to Religion," in Paul A. Schilpp (ed.), *The Philosophy of Karl Jaspers: A Critical Analysis and Evaluation* (New York: Tudor, 1957), pp. 611–42; and Jaspers, "Reply to My Critics," pp. 778–81 [A second,

apparent opposition to Jaspers' philosophical account of humankind's fundamental condition, Ricoeur contends that goodness, innocence, and freedom must be seen as more original than evil, guilt, and unfreedom.[56]

Ricoeur's (still untranslated) study *Gabriel Marcel et Karl Jaspers: philosophie du mystère et philosophie du paradoxe* constitutes an early and crucial instance of Ricoeur's dialectical thinking on the separation/relation, upon which my introduction remarks, between philosophy and religion. On the one hand, Ricoeur incorporates into his writing aspects of Jaspers' post-Kantian philosophy. He emphasizes that, consistent with Kant, transcendence involves the will's rebellion against heteronomous action which results from blind obedience to the dominating authority of religious institutions. Yet Jaspers' philosophical position, which recognizes paradoxical "ciphers" of transcendence, attempts to surpass what is perceived to be Kant's empty—i.e. overly formal—concept of human autonomy and postulates concerning pure practical reason.[57] The problem is that even the mere assumption of using God as a cipher of Transcendence is strongly criticized by, for one, Jaspers' contemporary Karl Barth,

> Far too often when a man says "God" he means by this cipher a mere something; that so-called "Transcendence"—empty, barren, and at bottom profoundly dull—which then, rather than as the true Opposite, the wholly and truthfully Other, the genuine Without and Beyond, will be much better interpreted as an illusionary reflection of human freedom, as its projection into a non-objective void.[58]

On the other hand, Ricoeur takes up Marcel's religious position, according to which the mysterious "gift" of transcendence constitutes a ground of hope and reflects the mystery of being, as the possible

---

augmented edition of this volume is published LaSalle, IL: Open Court Publishing Company, 1981].

[56] Ricoeur, *Fallible Man*, p. 222; *The Symbolism of Evil*, p. 156; and chapter three below.

[57] Ricoeur, *Gabriel Marcel et Karl Jaspers*, p. 420; and "*Interview avec Paul Ricoeur: Le 8 juillet 1991*," *Bulletin de la société américaine de philosophie de langue française*, pp. 155–57. As Jaspers himself explains, "To me the ciphers are suspended, to be questioned over and over; but in this suspension they are a language of the transcendent reality that meets the reality of Existenz" [Jaspers, *Philosophical Faith and Revelation*, trans. E.B. Ashton (London: Collins, 1967), p. 326]; also on ciphers of Transcendence, p. 95.

[58] Jaspers, *Philosophical Faith and Revelation*, p. 326; and Karl Barth, *Church Dogmatics*, vol. III, 2, trans. G. W. Bromiley and R. J. Ehrlich (Edinburgh: T and T Clark, 1960), pp. 113–20.

foundation of contemporary theology.[59] Ricoeur's appropriations of Jaspers and Marcel (who is nonetheless a Roman Catholic) seems to make possible a unique point of contact between Ricoeur's philosophical anthropology and his Protestant theology. However, even this connection may remain ambiguous insofar as Ricoeur continues to insist that his philosophy, including his secular use of Jaspers' transcendence, remains vehemently agnostic. In a retrospective interview Ricoeur explains,

> *le phénomène, l'expérience qui serait le plus près de l'expérience de la transcendence, comme l'expérience de la conscience morale, peut être interprétée de façon multiple. La conscience, comme voix intérieure, peut être celle de mes ancêtres, celle de mon être le plus profond comme le voudrait Heidegger, ou la parole d'un Dieu vivant. Mais, la philosophie laisse ouvertes ces possibilités. Et, c'est là que la jonction entre la dimension proprement philosophique et la dimension proprement religieuse intervient.*

> [the phenomenon or experience which would be the closest to the experience of transcendence, e.g. the experience of moral conscience, can be interpreted in various ways. The inner voice of conscience can be interpreted as the voice of my ancestors, as—Heidegger would interpret it—the voice of my most profound being, or as the word of a living God. But, philosophy leaves all these possibilities open. And yet, that is where the intersection between the properly philosophical dimension and the properly religious dimension occurs.][60]

Although I have endeavored to stress the distinctively French post-Kantian construction and reception of Ricoeur's philosophy, we must inevitably come up against a variety of ways in which his project is further informed by and informing modern Protestant theology. Various connections could be—and have been—made between Ricoeur's philosophical reflections and such different religious figures as, on the one hand, Sören Kierkegaard and Karl Barth and, on the other hand, Rudolf Bultmann and Jürgen Moltmann. These figures are essentially opposed according to their doctrines of God and human nature. Great disagreement has emerged in theological literature over the way in which Ricoeur's writings should be interpreted, especially, in relation

---

[59] Ibid., pp. 278–81, especially 276.

[60] "*Interview avec Paul Ricoeur*," p. 157. Also *Soi-même comme un autre*, pp. 36–37, 409; *Oneself as Another*, pp. 23–25, 355. There may be relationship between Ricoeur's philosophical agnosticism and his resistance to the Hegelian temptation of absolute knowledge (see below).

to the works of the twentieth-century theologians Karl Barth and Rudolf Bultmann.

For example, Lewis Mudge argues that Ricoeur is closer to Barth than Bultmann on the reception of a divine message, or experience of the divine, because Ricoeur "denies the notion of an independently existing conceptuality in us, ready to receive the message once it is demythologized, which plays so large a part in Bultmann's thought."[61] Also David Rasmussen points out that Bultmann maintains a distinction between the logical and the pre-logical which Ricoeur does not. Thus Ricoeur's interpretation of mythic-symbolic language differs from Bultmann's in such a way that his hermeneutics of symbols and myths concerning the sacred is not reductive as Bultmann's demythologising is said to be.[62]

Yet, clearly, interpreters of Ricoeur have taken strongly opposing viewpoints concerning his relationship to Barth. Herbert Spiegelberg claims that Ricoeur is repelled by Barth, while Loretta Dornisch and Peter Albano both emphasize, in their respective theological dissertations, the way in which Ricoeur is in accord with Barth.[63] In addition, William C. Placher has been adamant that Ricoeur is most definitely a Barthian; while David Klemm has more recently argued persuasively against Placher[64]—a similar position to that of Placher's is previously assumed by T.M. Van Leeuwen.[65]

Rather than comment in detail on Ricoeur's relationships to Barth and Bultmann I will turn to the more general, fundamental debt owed to Kant by all the previously named Protestant figures. Their debt is,

---

[61]   Lewis Mudge, "Paul Ricoeur on Biblical Interpretation," in Lewis Mudge (ed.), *Essays on Biblical Interpretation* (Philadelphia: Fortress Press, 1980), pp. 8–9.

[62]   David Rasmussen, *Mythic-Symbolic Language and Philosophical Anthropology: A Constructive Interpretation of the Thought of Paul Ricoeur* (The Hague: Martinus Nijhoff, 1971).

[63]   Herbert Spiegelberg, *The Phenomenological Movement*, II (The Hague: Martinus Nijhoff, 1960), pp. 563–78; Peter Albano, *Freedom, Truth and Hope: The Relation of Philosophy and Religion in the Thought of Paul Ricoeur*, PhD Dissertation (Calif.: Claremont Graduate School, 1976); and Loretta Dornisch, *A Theological Interpretation of the Meaning of Symbol in the Theory of Paul Ricoeur and Possible Implications for Contemporary Education*, PhD Dissertation (Marquette University, 1973).

[64]   David Klemm, "Ricoeur, Theology and the Rhetoric of Overturning," *Literature and Theology*, vol. 3, no. 3 (November 1989), pp. 267–284. Klemm carefully develops Ricoeur's relationship to Heidegger and Bultmann but only makes one passing reference to Barth in *The Hermeneutical Theory of Paul Ricoeur: A Constructive Analysis* (London/Toronto: Associated University Press, 1983).

[65]   Van Leeuwen, *The Surplus of Meaning*.

however, precarious because Kant radically challenges the cognitive foundation of traditional theology. Consequently nineteenth-century and twentieth-century theologians are forced to confront the implications of Kant's critiques of theoretical knowledge of self, God, and the end of all things. Furthermore we should recall—with regard to Kant's ideas of reasons, namely, of freedom, God, and immortality—McCarthy's question, "are Kant's ideas of reason illusions of logocentric thinking that must tirelessly be deconstructed…?" In order to answer McCarthy and to foreground Ricoeur's critical relationship to contemporary theologians I continue to elucidate his particular Kantian standpoint.

III. A Post-Hegelian Kantian Standpoint

In "Freedom in the Light of Hope," Ricoeur acknowledges that the self-description of his standpoint as post-Hegelian Kantian is actually taken from Eric Weil.[66] Ricoeur explains that this Kantianism is "more to be constructed than repeated."[67] And we have already recognized that Ricoeur's project aims to construct a philosophy of the will. In his attempt to construct this philosophy Ricoeur reconsiders, in "Freedom in the Light of Hope," the significance of Kant's practical postulates concerning human freedom, God, and immortality. For Ricoeur, Kant's postulates preserve human rationality in general, as well as the actual contingent realms of human experience; the postulates are deduced transcendentally as presuppositions of our rational thought and action, as well as limitations on our theoretical knowledge. Insisting that such postulates, or ideas of reason, serve in this way as Kantian limiting concepts for his thought, Ricoeur claims to set Kant's unresolved dialectics of theoretical and practical reason against Hegel's totalizing dialectics of absolute knowledge.[68] Subsequent chapters say much more about Ricoeur's philosophy as it is constructed within Kantian limits and so sustains a fundamental duality—despite an interaction—between freedom and nature, reason and experience. At this point we should understand that his post-Hegelian Kantian standpoint is a result of

---

[66] Ricoeur, "Freedom in the Light of Hope," trans. Robert Sweeney, *The Conflict of Interpretations*, pp. 412–15; cf. Eric Weil, *Problèmes kantiens*, p. 33.

[67] Ibid.

[68] See chapter two for my discussion concerning Ricoeur's use of Kant's *Grenzbegriff* ("limit concept").

moving from the phenomenology of Hegel back to the limits set by Kant's critical philosophy.[69]

We might contextualize this move in relation to Weil,

> Weil's "interest" in Kant and in moral philosophy generally expressed his effort to find "a reason to hope." A major facet of the pretension of Hegelianism for Weil was the idea that such a reason could be found in, or was identical with, history. This idea came to seem pretentious as the confidence that persons brought to history diminished ... Weil's pronounced Kantian [re]turn was an attempt to uncover the point of this labor or at least to find in the storm of history a shelter that was more than a retreat to isolated particularity.[70]

The decisive question, which leads both Weil and Ricoeur to supplement Hegel with a return to Kant, is: How do we account for the particularity and contingency of the human subject? For Weil it is reason embodied in language which saves us from the extremes of either totalization and loss of our particularity or isolation and loss of any hope for a meaningful unity to human history. On this point Weil brings to mind the more well-known German philosopher Jürgen Habermas, whose rationality of communicative action might be close to what Weil wants to envisage by reason embodied in language.[71] This point is relevant for Ricoeur since, to reiterate, the post-Hegelian Kantian standpoint, which he tries to establish along with such others as Weil and Habermas, aims to preserve rationality in general without giving up actual contingent realms of our temporal experience. Put more simply, the standpoint intends to retain the general and the particular, the non-temporal and the temporal, by relating the universal and the individual in human history. In the next chapter this standpoint will be elaborated in terms of the dual-aspect—rational and sensible—subject.

Initially, and still to a degree today, we can see that Hegel serves a crucial function in the development of Ricoeur's thought concerning reason in general and its relation to the contingent realm of objects. Already at the early stage of his phenomenological analysis of willing, Ricoeur confronts the dualism between subject and object; he reads this

---

[69]   Ricoeur, "Freedom in the Light of Hope," pp. 412–24.

[70]   Roth, *Knowing and History*, p. 180.

[71]   Jürgen Habermas, *Communication and the Evolution of Society*, trans. Thomas McCarthy (Boston: Beacon Press, 1979), pp. 117, 119–120; and Ricoeur, *Soi-même comme un autre*, pp. 257, 325–29; *Oneself as Another*, pp. 221, 280–83. Cf. John B. Thompson, *Critical Hermeneutics: A Study in the Thought of Paul Ricoeur and Jürgen Habermas* (Cambridge: Cambridge University Press, 1981).

dualism in terms of the voluntary and the involuntary moments of consciousness which are given orientation in history by an ideal unity. As he explains,

> In the particular case of the phenomenology of the will it seems to me that the study of the articulations between the voluntary and the involuntary moments of consciousness is constantly orientated by the ideal of the unity of the human person. It is very striking that it should be precisely the great dualisms of history which have most prized this unity, as if dualism were the philosophical test one had to pass through in order to conquer the true meaning of unity.[72]

We should keep in mind Ricoeur's reference to "the ideal of the unity of the human person"; this ideal will be gradually elucidated in post-Hegelian Kantian terms as we come to understand Ricoeur's use of the two-Adams myths.

It is illuminating for us that Ricoeur also describes his standpoint as post-Hegelian Kantian in his "Fatherhood: From Phantasm to Symbol."[73] In this characteristic essay Ricoeur claims to confront the Freudian critique of God as Father by way of a post-Hegelian Kantian style of concrete reflection; and to use Hegel's phenomenology of the will as a philosophical instrument to throw light on the conflict of theological and psychoanalytic interpretations of God as Father. His interpretation of the figure of the father intends a mediation between psychoanalysis and religion. His mediating analysis of the father follows Hegel's phenomenology of the will in developing a dialectic between the will of the father and the will of the son. The intention, as above, is to relate the subject and object, the universal and individual in history, and so to avoid the loss of a meaningful unity as a reason to hope. In this case Ricoeur explains,

> the philosophical strength of the analysis... points toward a theology of hope without, however, necessarily implying it. Remove this [phenomenology of the will] and the analysis is undone or destroys itself in insoluble conflicts; many confrontations between psychoanalysis and religion are badly directed and badly controlled for lack of this

---

[72] Ricoeur, "The Antinomy of Human Reality and the Problem of Philosophical Anthropology," p. 2.

[73] Ricoeur, "Fatherhood: From Phantasm to Symbol," trans. Robert Sweeney, *The Conflict of Interpretations*, pp. 468–97.

philosophical instrument and the mediation exercised by what I call concrete reflection.[74]

Still it is not easy to grasp the full significance of this concrete reflection; again it is helpful to recognize the intellectual context which informs Ricoeur's reflections.

We have already recognized that Weil attends Kojève's lectures on Hegel's *Phenomenology of Spirit*; and that the general impact of Kojève's lectures becomes evident in certain works of French intellectuals between 1933 and 1968. Notably Merleau-Ponty's existential phenomenology, Sartre's phenomenological ontology, and Ricoeur's hermeneutic phenomenology reflect the distinctively French reading of Hegel which emerges during this period of time. Kojève makes Hegel's master and slave dialectic the key to his interpretation of the *Phenomenology*; following suit, the 1930s generation in Paris never cease to refer to Hegel's master/slave dialectic.[75] Ricoeur is consistent on this; and so for insight we can turn to his concrete reflection upon Hegel's renowned dialectic.

From "Independence and Dependence of Self-consciousness: Lordship and Bondage" in Hegel's *Phenomenology*, Ricoeur would assume that consciousness exists for itself (i.e. the truth of independent self-consciousness exists) only when its autonomy is recognized by another consciousness.[76] Following Hegel, a subject is constituted in self-consciousness by another subject in being recognized by this other and recognizes the other as recognising it. In the master and slave dialectic, the master at first succeeds at obtaining recognition by imposing himself or herself as the other's value; the slave is the subject who sees his or her own true value in the other. However, a contradiction lies concealed in this initial situation. It must be conceded that the subject in bondage is not recognized as a real person. In addition, being dependent on the slave for recognition means that the master deprives himself or herself of the freedom which is required for the development of genuine self-consciousness. Ironically the master is not free but in bondage to his or

---

[74] Ibid., p. 496.

[75] Descombes, *Modern French Philosophy*, pp. 22–23.

[76] Ricoeur, "Fatherhood: From Phantasm to Symbol," pp. 471–81; *Lectures on Ideology and Utopia*, pp. 227–31, 241; and *Soi-même comme un autre*, p. 407; *Oneself as Another*, p. 353. Cf. Hegel, *Phenomenology of Spirit*, pp. 111–19; Kojève, *Introduction to the Reading of Hegel*, pp. 3–30; and Roth, *Knowing and History*, pp. 109–17.

her slave. The truth of self-consciousness has to be found in the independent consciousness which is for itself.

In "Independence and Dependence of Self-consciousness," Hegel portrays the process in which mutual recognition is reached as a life and death struggle. Death is identified as the absolute master who throws the trembling subject entirely upon himself or herself alone. The life and death struggle consists in the fact that the slave, in the fear of death, externalizes himself or herself for the master in work on the reality of things. By reshaping reality the subject who works comes to view independent being as itself. And consciousness of the subject in bondage becomes aware through the rediscovery of himself or herself by himself or herself, of having and being a "mind of its own" (*eigener Sinn*), in the labor in which it had previously seemed to be merely some "outsider's mind" (*fremder Sinn*).[77] Yet the freedom of consciousness consists not only in the confirmation of self given in existent things but also in successful self-assertion in opposition to dependency on life. In the total dissolution of self-consciousness in the face of death the being-for-self becomes a new form of self-consciousness, i.e. a consciousness which is free. This means being able, in disregard of oneself, to accept as valid that confrontation with death in which no single self can consider himself or herself superior to another. At this point Hegel's dialectic reaches the stage where the subject and the other recognize themselves as mutually recognising one another. Up to this point, at least, Ricoeur would accept our reading of Hegel.

But, in a loose interpretation of Hegel's text, Kojève begins his seminars on the *Phenomenology* by asking, "What is the Hegelian person?"—a question which subsequently preoccupies French intellectuals including Ricoeur. Kojève's answer is both to give an account of desire and to make this account concrete by developing a master and slave story. In his account, Kojève draws a distinction between human desire and animal desire; and so he introduces into Hegel a dualism which is *not* present in the *Phenomenology*.[78] According

---

77 Hegel, *Phenomenology*, p. 119.
78 For a much more detailed discussion of Kojève's appropriation of Hegel's doctrine of desire see Judith Butler, *Subjects of Desire: Hegelian Reflections in Twentieth-Century France* (New York: Columbia University Press, 1987), pp. 62–79. Butler is especially helpful in explaining Kojève's rejection of Hegel's premise of ontological harmony as that which conditions and resolves all experience of difference between individual humans, and between humans and the external world; ibid., pp. 63, 65–66, 69–71.

to Kojève's Hegel, then, human desire is the desire for recognition, which alone can lead to self-consciousness; human desire has as its object another desire and not another thing as is the object of animal desire. Also animal desire draws one to the body of another, but human desire expresses the wish to be desired, loved or recognized by another. For Kojève's Hegel there is a crucial conflict between human desire and animal desire; the latter aims to preserve the life of an individual, while the former is not necessarily attached to objects which continue life. For instance, human desire is evident in one's willingness to risk one's life for the sake of some form of recognition, to decide self-consciously it is better to die than to live without the satisfaction which comes from recognition.[79]

In developing a story out of Hegel's master and slave dialectic, Kojève makes concrete his distinction between human and animal desires. Kojève's story rereads the three moments of Hegel's dialectic as the bloody battle, the reign of the master and the triumph of the slave. For Kojève the loser of the bloody battle is really the one who decides that life is more important than the recognition originally sought; the loser allows the animal desire for self-preservation to win out over the human desire for recognition. When the slave works for the master, while the master enjoys the fruits of the slave, the victory of the master is only apparent. Under the reign of the master, the work of the slave satisfies the animal desires of the master. Yet the master lacks the recognition which produces Hegelian self-certainty, since the slave's self cannot really recognize the master. For Kojève the hierarchy of master and slave prohibits the satisfaction of properly human desire. In fact the position of the master is an *impasse existentiale* according to Kojève, whereas the slave's actions constitute the crucial seed of historical development. Fear and work are the determining motivations of the slave's actions and so of history; the (slave's) fear of the master is only the beginning of wisdom.[80]

Ultimately for Kojève the dynamic of mastery and slavery provides the drama and driving force of history: domination sets history in motion but only equality will end it. In Kojève's reading of Hegel, social and political perspectives have priority over personal and psychological alienation, which take precedence in Jean Hyppolite's emphasis on the

---

[79] Kojève, *Introduction to the Reading of Hegel*, pp. 6–7.
[80] Ibid., p. 29; cf. Hegel, *Phenomenology*, pp. 117–18.

unhappy consciousness in Hegel's *Phenomenology*.[81] Moreover, for Kojève's Hegel, Christianity becomes the crucial stage for the slave in affirming freedom and equality. The triumph of the slave is the victory of equality over hierarchy; in Christianity the concept of the individual is linked to equality: the individual is a synthesis of the universal (divine) and the particular (profane). Kojève realizes that the idea of incarnation is the most powerful image of this synthesis, since the universal assumes the corporeal form of a particular man: God is an individual. The "truth" of Christianity for Kojève's Hegel lies in its incarnation; Christian love is realized through historical action; and love can only exist between equals, in mutual recognition.[82] Yet for Kojève, in sharp contrast with Ricoeur at this point, the becoming of atheism is the process of liberation from God as the absolute master; and this becoming is the acknowledgement of the universal equality of individuals. Our initial freedom, which is our historical freedom, lies in our ability to negate, to initiate change through struggle and work. And this ability is a product of our human desire for recognition. With the achievement of equality comes the satisfaction of the slave and this satisfaction is a sort of death. To conclude on Kojève's Hegel, his reading of the *Phenomenology* is characterized by violence and negation; as a posthistorical reading, Kojève's has been called the "humanization of nothingness."[83]

Before returning to Ricoeur's post-Hegelian reading of fatherhood and sonship, we should be able to realize from the above that the French readings of Hegel, whether that of Kojève, Hyppolite, Weil, or Ricoeur, do not seek a precise analysis of Hegel's argument in the *Phenomenology*. Instead they each seek in Hegel philosophical answers to specific political, social, personal, and/or theological questions concerning human history, reason, and self-identity—questions which in fact reflect those years of intellectual struggle in Europe between 1933 and 1968. It is in this light that we can understand the way in which the philosophical interpretation of the will, which Ricoeur finds in Hegel, enables him to reconstruct the fundamental relation of fatherhood and sonship and so to confront Freud (and, by implication, Kojève's Hegel). Ricoeur maintains that once the father, who is similar to the master in Hegel's dialectic, is recognized as a member of a living community, then fatherhood can be transformed from a phantasm—i.e. a Freudian illusion—to a symbol. For

---

[81]   As noted in my introduction Jean Hyppolite offers the other, existential French reading of Hegel; Hyppolite, *Genesis and Structure of Hegel's Phenomenology of Spirit*.

[82]   Kojève, *Introduction to the Reading of Hegel*, p. 55.

[83]   Descombes, *Modern French Philosophy*, pp. 9–48.

Ricoeur the symbol of fatherhood would bring together the dual intentionalities of life, as in the satisfaction of Kojève's animal desire, and of love or mutual recognition, as in the satisfaction of Kojève's human desire.[84]

Rather cryptically perhaps, Ricoeur explains his own movement from Freud to Hegel to Kant as connected by the symbolism of a kingdom. Ricoeur relates his discussion of mutual recognition—of father and of son—to the category of the kingdom of God. It is Kant who first treats this category as a limiting concept in the second *Critique*, then, as a symbol in *Religion within the Limits of Reason Alone*. Ricoeur's exact statement is:

> We can say: from phantasm to symbol ... from non-recognized fatherhood, mortal and mortifying for desire, to recognized fatherhood which has become the tie between love and life.
>
> ...For my own part I feel myself closer to Kant finally—to the Kant of *Religion within the Limits of Reason Alone*—than to Hegel.
>
> ...It is on the basis of this category of the kingdom that we must interpret the category of father. Eschatological royalty and fatherhood remain inseparable.[85]

Having become acquainted with the essential French context for Ricoeur's readings of Hegel and Kant, we should be able to imagine the manner in which recognized fatherhood, for Ricoeur, might constitute the concrete structure of the kingdom of God. We will find that, in the end, Kant provides the conceptual framework to make the structure intelligible.

Now in order to introduce the theological significance of Ricoeur's post-Hegelian Kantian structure for the kingdom of God let us bring in the contemporary German theologian Jürgen Moltmann. Like Ricoeur, Moltmann finds his intellectual provenance in the philosophies of Kant and Hegel.[86] That Ricoeur's reflections are at points intellectually

---

[84] Ricoeur, "Fatherhood: From Phantasm to Symbol," pp. 474–81; cf. *Freud and Philosophy*, pp. 462–77.

[85] Ibid., pp. 481, 490.

[86] It should be noted, however, that Moltmann assumes different possible meanings for the kingdom of God: as a present historical reality, as a socialist idea of a future utopia and as the promise of an eschatological other-worldly transformation of the Christian community. See Moltmann, *Theology of Hope: On the Ground and the Implications of a Christian Eschatology*, trans. James W. Leitch (London: SCM, 1967) and *The Crucified God: The Cross of Christ as the Foundation and Criticism of Christian Theology*, trans. R. A. Wilson and John Bowden (London: SCM, 1974).

compatible with Moltmann's theology is attested to by the former's own acknowledged debt to the latter's *Theology of Hope*.[87] Not only is Ricoeur definitely informed by Moltmann but Moltmann makes references to Ricoeur's "La liberté selon l'espérance."[88]

It is especially relevant for a discussion regarding the post-Hegelian Kantian contexts of Ricoeur's writings that, in the first chapter of his *Theology of Hope*, Moltmann traces the modern confusion concerning the eschatological meaning of the kingdom of God back to Kant's critiques. Moltmann maintains that Kant led modern theologians to conceive of a transcendental eschatology, an expression which needs to be understood in the light of Kant's "The End of All Things."[89] In this short treatise, Kant subjects the eighteenth-century Christian doctrine of eschatology to a radical critique, the essence of which is that there can be no such thing as theoretical knowledge of the last things; these objects must lie wholly beyond our spatio-temporal experience. Kant argues that

> We are dealing (or playing) here simply with Ideas which reason itself creates, the objects of which (if it possesses any) lie completely beyond our field of vision; and although these Ideas are transcendent for our speculative cognition, they are still not on that account to be considered void in all respects. Made available to us by the legislative reason itself, these Ideas are to be regarded rather in a practical sense, not laboriously pondered with respect to their objects, whatever these are in and of themselves and according to their nature, but rather as we are required to contemplate them on behalf of the moral principles which pertain to the ultimate purpose of all things.[90]

Kant's critique of the end of all things forces certain theologians to develop a transcendental eschatology of moral principles pertaining to the end of all things. And this means that, after Kant, the *eschata* are understood to be the transcendental conditions for the possibility of experiencing either one's moral self-fulfilment or God's self-revelation in a practical way. This critique applies to any conceivable eschatology expressed in terms of the spatio-temporal history of the kingdom of God. Moltmann, for instance, insists:

---

87 Ricoeur, *Essays on Biblical Interpretation*, p. 157.
88 Moltmann "Liberation in the Light of Hope," (1974), p. 420; and "God with the Human Face," in Elisabeth Moltmann-Wendel and Jürgen Moltmann, *Humanity in God* (London: SCM Press, 1984), p. 67.
89 Moltmann, *Theology of Hope*, pp. 45–50.
90 Kant, "The End of All Things," in Lewis Beck (ed.), *On History*, trans. R. E. Anchor, (New York: Macmillan, 1985), pp. 75–76.

The classical philosophical form of transcendental eschatology is found in Immanuel Kant. Its basic features recur wherever Kantian thinking is found in the revelational theology of modern times.[91]

And this transcendental eschatology appears in Ricoeur as well as, however distinctively, in the revelational theologies of Barth and Bultmann.

Recalling "Freedom in the Light of Hope," the essay with which we began this section, Ricoeur claims that the freedom revealed in Christian Scripture has an individual expression and, even more, a communitarian, historical and political expression in the expectation of universal resurrection.[92] This claim reflects Ricoeur's Kantian thought concerning transcendental eschatology as ground of hope, as well as his affinity with revelational theologies. In particular Ricoeur explains that this freedom is revealed, according to a certain logic of superabundance, in the figure of Christ in the New Testament and given symbolic expression by the first and second Adams. Ricoeur derives a typology from the analogy between Christ and Adam found in *Romans* 5:12–21.

In support of his typology of the first and second Adams, Ricoeur's "The Image of God and the Epic of Man" makes reference to Karl Barth's "Christ and Adam: Man and Humanity in *Romans* 5."[93] Barth uses the anti-type, Adam, to represent the sin of humankind; this anti-type can only be understood in the light of the type of the second Adam, Christ, who represents "...the grace of God and the gift of this grace coming from one man—Christ Jesus—which "has abounded for many."[94] As Barth writes

> ...the new point is that the *special* anthropology of Jesus Christ—the one man for all men, all men in the one man—constitutes the secret of "Adam" also, and so is the norm of all anthropology.[95]

In *The Symbolism of Evil*, Ricoeur employs an exegetical analogy in his reading of the Adamic myth.[96] Ricoeur's reading assumes that the

---

91 Moltmann, *Theology of Hope*, p. 46.
92 Ricoeur, "Freedom in the Light of Hope," p. 411.
93 Ricoeur, *History and Truth*, p. 120; cf. Karl Barth, "Christ and Adam: Man and Humanity in *Romans* 5," trans. T. A. Small, *Scottish Journal of Theology*, Occasional Paper No. 5 (1956).
94 Barth, ibid., p. 5.
95 Ibid.
96 By using this analogy to portray the ideal human Ricoeur restricts himself to male symbolism. In this context *l'homme* unequivocally means man.

analogical relationship represented by the two-Adams typology links the Old and New Testaments, as well as the one man and all men. Adam, the anti-type, is known in retrospect through Christ's self-revelation as the type, human and divine. We recall that Ricoeur's Kantian limiting concept makes impossible any straightforward claim to knowledge of God. However Ricoeur speaks in Kantian terms of a schematism of analogy which serves in practical knowledge of the second Adam or Christ. We will find that he also refers to "the schematization of the good principle" (*le schématisme du Bon Principe*)[97] and the "schematization of the archetype in Christ" (*le schématisme de l'Archétype de l'homme dans Christ*).[98]

The schematism as a procedure of the pure productive imagination, the use of which I will continue to illustrate, is presented in Kant's first *Critique*; there the schematism determines the non-temporal in terms of time by offering an image, or set of images, to mediate the universal and individual. In his *Religion*, Kant also claims that a schematism of analogy functions for practical knowledge of the archetype, Christ.[99]

The crucial question is: How close does Ricoeur's schematization of the universal—the non-temporal—in the archetype, as reflected in his typology of the two Adams, come to Hegel's account of time and eternity? We can recall that even Kojève, the atheist, sees the "truth" of Hegel's image of the incarnation in Christian love which can only exist between equals, that is, in love's synthesis of the universal or divine (and so by definition eternal) and the particular or profane (and so temporal). For Hegel, in this light, time and eternity come together in the incarnation of the universal in the historical action of an individual man. For Ricoeur, in apparent contrast, any and all synthesis between time and eternity remain unresolved since, following Kant he repeatedly claims that such synthesis is unresolvable.[100] Yet Ricoeur continues to struggle with the great temptation of Hegel's thought. This temptation could be

---

[97] Ricoeur, "Freedom in the Light of Hope," p. 424.

[98] Ricoeur, *Le Conflit des interprétations: Essais d'herméneutique*, I (Paris: Editions du Seuil, 1969), pp. 414–15n; *The Conflict of Interpretations*, p. 424n. Cf. Kant, *Religion within the limits of Reason Alone*, trans. Theodore Greene and Hoyt Hudson (New York: Harper and Row, 1960), pp. 56–59.

[99] See previous footnote. However, ultimately for Ricoeur, the revelation of God in Christ depends upon a hermeneutic of revelation; that is a concept of revelation which is "pluralistic, polysemic and at most analogical in form." Ricoeur, "Toward a Hermeneutic of the Idea of Revelation," in Lewis Mudge (ed.), *Essays on Biblical Interpretation*, pp. 73–118, especially 75.

[100] See footnote 49 above.

explained in postmodern terms as the desire to construct a totalizing grand narrative.[101] As Ricoeur—rather cryptically—admits

> Ought we not decipher... the symptom of a kind of thinking that has not dared to elevate itself to grasping history as the totalization of time in the eternal present?
> From this question comes the Hegelian temptation.[102]

Consistent with Ricoeur's temptation to the totalization of time in the eternal present are his claims that, first, "between [Hegel's] absolute knowledge and hermeneutics it is necessary to choose" and that, second, "the conflict of interpretations is insurmountable."[103] So Ricoeur chooses hermeneutics over absolute knowledge, which means that he never ultimately overcomes conflicting interpretations of history, of time and its relation to eternity. In his philosophy of the will Ricoeur continually re-assesses the relationship of human time and primordial time or, in some cases, of time and eternity. His continual re-interpretation of temporal experience is apparent in his mythical re-enactments—in a second *naiveté*[104]—of experiences of evil and innocence, and especially, in narrative refigurations concerning sin and salvation. Despite his resistance to the Hegelian temptation of totalization and absolute knowledge, it might be asked whether or not Ricoeur's reflections achieve an original, mediating position between Hegel and Kant on how to read human history in terms of time and eternity. He is still discussing this problem in *Time and Narrative*, III; in "Interpretative Narrative" he addresses the Hegelian temptation with reference to the narrative mediation of the infra-temporal and supra-temporal.[105]

---

[101] Jean-François Lyotard, *The Postmodern Condition: A Report on Knowledge*, trans. George Van Den Abbeele (Mpls: University of Minnesota Press, 1988), pp. 33–37.

[102] Ricoeur, "Should We Renounce Hegel?" *Time and Narrative*, III, p. 193, also 193–206, 258ff.

[103] Ricoeur, *Hermeneutics and the Human Sciences*, p. 193.

[104] Ricoeur, *The Symbolism of Evil*, pp. 351–53.

[105] Ricoeur, *Time and Narrative*, III, pp. 103, 193–206; and "Interpretative Narrative," in Roberta Schwartz (ed.), *The Book and the Text* (Oxford: Basil Blackwell, 1990), pp. 237–57; cf. G.W. F. Hegel, *Lectures on the Philosophy of World History: Introduction—Reason in History*, trans. Duncan Forbes (Cambridge: Cambridge University Press, 1975).

IV. Kant and The Hermeneutics of Suspicion

At this stage we should leave the question of Ricoeur's success in avoiding Hegelian idealism in order to consider the way in which his return to Kant informs a hermeneutics of suspicion—as a potential critique of any absolute idealism. In the previous section we saw that Kant's philosophical critique of the doctrine of the last things contributes to Ricoeur's reading of the kingdom of God. At the same time as being critical of theoretical knowledge of the end of all things Kant, in his *Religion*, also provides crucial ground for the possibility of a transcendental eschatology. In fact Ricoeur's post-Hegelian Kantian reading of eschatology, based upon freedom in the light of hope, both distinguishes him from and relates him to other contemporary Protestant theologians, notably to Barth, Bultmann, and Moltmann. Kant's critiques force each of these modern theologians to develop distinctive practical realizations of Christian eschatology.

Considering the potential eschatology in Kant before Ricoeur, the *Religion* presents essentially two possible accounts of the kingdom of God. The first might be called the religious account; the second is an account of the social significance of the concept of the kingdom of God. The religious interpretation of Kant's use of this concept involves the inner transformation of the believer's will and the hope of the union of all believers with God who remains sovereign over the human, natural, and moral worlds as creator, judge, and ruler.

The social significance of the kingdom of God emerges according to a particular reading of the *Religion* which finds that Kant's account of hope suggests a this-worldly progress toward *summum bonum* or, as discussed in the next chapter, the highest good. Such a view of the kingdom of God with reference to actual social progress places hope in the perfect coordination of happiness and virtue as represented by the regulative idea or the postulate of God. In this account the social significance of the kingdom of God is, then, an immanent possibility whose significance for Christians does not depend on any transcendent or subjective claims concerning God. On the contrary, it depends upon a moral—i.e. Kantian[106]—interpretation of Judaeo-Christian scriptures and a non-transcendent interpretation of the crucial symbols of the incarnation, crucifixion, and resurrection of Christ.

---

[106] For an interpretation of Kant's moral philosophy which brings out the anthropological-social significance of his *Religion*, see Agnes Heller, *Beyond Justice* (Oxford: Basil Blackwell, 1987), pp. 94–106.

These comments concerning two different readings of a Kantian kingdom of God inform the attempt to answer the question of where Ricoeur stands with reference to eschatology. Ricoeur's philosophy of the will definitely incorporates Kant's discussions of hope and his postulates of pure practical reason into its account of the relationship between God and man or woman.[107] Ricoeur's interpretation aims to mediate the social and religious meanings of the kingdom of God. His endeavor to achieve such mediation is significant for the theological and hermeneutical implications of Ricoeur's philosophy of the will.

In order to recognize Ricoeur's mediating interpretation of the kingdom of God in its contribution to a critical hermeneutics, it is important to re-read his "Religion, Atheism, and Faith." Here Ricoeur reconstructs the kind of faith that is possible after Freud's and Nietzsche's respective critiques of the moral God of Kant. This essay exhibits the potentially radical element of Ricoeur's deconstruction,[108] or critical thought, and reconstruction, or restorative criticism, of the Judaeo-Christian concept of God—as an indirect answer to McCarthy's question on deconstructing one of Kant's three ideas of reason. Ricoeur claims that Freud and Nietzsche force the contemporary theologian to "dig…until one reaches the level of questioning that makes possible a mediation between religion and faith by means of atheism."[109] The critiques of Freud and Nietzsche are seen to be far more radical than Kant's epistemological critique of God. As Ricoeur explains,

> with Kant…and finally with Nietzsche himself, humankind as subject becomes humankind as will. The will appears as the origin of values, while the world retires into the background as simple fact, deprived of all value. Nihilism is not far distant.
>   …we must now return to a point that is situated prior to the dichotomy between subject and object.[110]

Ricoeur argues that, first, Kant attempts to reconcile freedom and nature with his postulates of practical reason under the rule of a moral

---

[107] Ricoeur, "Freedom in the Light of Hope," pp. 418–22.

[108] Ricoeur's references to deconstruction are not to be confused with Derrida's more technical textual strategy. See Ricoeur, "Fatherhood: From Phantasm to Symbol," p. 482; "Philosophical Hermeneutics and Biblical Hermeneutics," in *From Text to Action*, pp. 100–1; also footnote 7 above.

[109] Ricoeur, "Religion, Atheism, and Faith," trans. Charles Freilich, in *The Conflict of Interpretations*, p. 460; this essay is written in 1966 during the time when Ricoeur's volumes on the will are being translated into English.

[110] Ibid., p. 463.

God. Next, Hegel criticizes Kant's moral vision of the world, but proceeds to construct a rational system in which all contradictions are reconciled. Finally, Nietzsche contends that the will which is hidden behind the rationalizations of both Kant and Hegel is always a weak will. In this regard Ricoeur maintains that

> Our critique of metaphysics and its search for rational reconciliation must give way to a positive ontology...[which] consists in an entirely non-ethical vision, or what Nietzsche described as "the innocence of becoming."[111]

This non-ethical vision, or Nietzsche's innocence of becoming, implies criticism of both Kant and Hegel.[112] Yet Ricoeur retains his fundamental Kantian emphasis on the dialectics of theoretical and practical reason and the postulates of pure practical reason. At the same time, he calls for a return to the roots of the Judaeo-Christian faith. His radical concept is of "...a God who would not protect me but would surrender me to the dangers of a life worthy of being called human."[113] This concept of God still provides, in Ricoeur's post-Hegelian Kantian terms, the ground of ontological and eschatological hope.

Ricoeur must assume that, as I will emphasize later, Kant also both retains an anthropology which is fundamentally Judaeo-Christian and foreshadows the critiques of Marx, Nietzsche, and Freud. It seems to be assumed—rightly—that according to Kant any knowledge of a noumenal self, of God, or of the thing-in-itself is impossible. In his *Critique of Pure Reason*, Kant argues that there can only be knowledge of phenomena and so I can have knowledge of my phenomenal self, but no knowledge of a noumenal self—except the negative knowledge that myself as an object of thought cannot be known in-itself—is possible for a dual-aspect being. In Kant's words,

> I, as intelligence and *thinking* [*denkend*] subject...know myself, like other phenomena, only as I appear to myself, not as I am to the understanding.[114]

However, Kant also maintains that human reason continues to seek knowledge of the unconditioned, i.e. of human freedom, God, and the

---

[111] Ibid., p. 457.

[112] These criticisms could be developed. In this regard I refer the reader to Gilles Deleuze's more radical use of Nietzsche in developing an anti-dialectical—even postmodern —position over and against both Kant and Hegel; Deleuze, *Nietzsche and Philosophy*, p. 9.

[113] Ricoeur, "Religion, Atheism, and Faith," p. 460.

[114] Kant, *Critique of Pure Reason*, B155.

thing-in-itself. It is precisely because human reason always desires the unconditioned that transcendental illusion is inevitable. This is to say that we continually deceive ourselves.[115] In more modern terms, Kant's critique of transcendental illusion reveals a false consciousness. Such critique of inevitable illusion and false consciousness allows us to say that Kant foreshadows the masters of suspicion—Marx, Nietzsche, and Freud—and their respective critiques of ideology, morality, and immediate self-consciousness. I contend that it is only with this critical interpretation of Kant that Ricoeur may be understood in his assuming that contemporary theologians, after confronting the modern hermeneuticists of suspicion, should return to Kant in order to reconstruct symbolically such concepts of Judaeo-Christian theology as that of the kingdom of God. Nevertheless, by way of an internal critique, I will also show that Ricoeur's post-Kantian account of human experience itself can become the object of a hermeneutics of suspicion.

Allow me to illustrate the way in which a hermeneutics of suspicion can be turned back upon Ricoeur's own project. One contemporary attempt at radical criticism and restoration of the traditional concept of God as Father is, for example, represented by Mary Daly in her early work, *Beyond God the Father*.[116] Addressing fundamental questions such as those approached by Ricoeur in "Fatherhood: From Phantasm to Symbol" and "Religion, Atheism, and Faith," albeit in a feminist context, Daly intends to destroy both the idols constructed by cultural institutions and the illusions constituted by human knowledge. The early Daly illustrates for us the significance of the iconoclasm which critiques formulated by even radical feminists and atheists can offer to contemporary thought as hermeneutics of suspicion. In a manner not foreign to a critical hermeneuticist, Daly uncovers three idolatrous, patriarchal images of God: "the God of explanation," "the God of other-worldliness," and God as "the Judge of sin" who confirms the rightness of the rules and roles of the reigning political-economic system. The early Daly, then, criticizes these images and claims instead that the authentic image of God is the creative potential in human beings. In order for this creative potential to be recognized in women, as well as in men, these three philosophically-defined idols of God which reinforce male superiority and patriarchy must be destroyed. We could, quite easily, redirect Daly's feminist contentions concerning patriarchal symbolism

---

[115] Ibid., A297–98/B354–55.
[116] Daly, *Beyond God the Father: Toward a Philosophy of Women's Liberation* (Boston: Beacon Press, 1973; London: The Woman's Press, 1986), pp. 29–31.

against Ricoeur's post-Hegelian Kantian category of fatherhood, as well as against his ideal typology of the first and second Adam.[117] And yet Ricoeur's characteristic willingness to confront modern critiques of theology leaves open the possibility that, if seriously and appropriately confronted by such feminist critique, he would attempt to transform exclusively male aspects of his thought.[118]

Sallie McFague, another woman philosopher/theologian, who however different from Daly, follows her in questioning the symbol of God as Father; and, in addition, McFague claims to appropriate Ricoeur's work on metaphor.[119] In *Metaphorical Theology*, McFague identifies idolatry and irrelevance, respectively, as the two crucial problems of contemporary literal and positivistic descriptions of God. She refers to Daly's criticisms of God conceived of as Father and to the increasing number of feminist critiques of the traditional Judaeo-Christian conception of God. Yet it is in my opinion unfortunate that McFague's particular emphasis upon the power of metaphor to express imaginatively, which means for her unconventionally, the kingdom of God remains merely an attempt to overcome a positivistic stranglehold and the accompanying conventional talk of God.[120] For a project to be more consistent with the *potentially* radical aspects in Ricoeur, it would have to seek a fundamental critique of the religious, social, and cultural symbols which are thought to be constitutive of the self-consciousness of humanity.[121] With this reference to self-consciousness in Ricoeur we should now turn to ask: Who exactly constitutes humanity?

---

[117] Jacqueline Field-Bibb directs feminist criticism against Ricoeur in her *Women Towards the Priesthood: Ministerial Politics and Feminist Praxis* (Cambridge: Cambridge University Press, 1991), pp. 248–49, 265–67 and 287–89. In an earlier article, "'By Any Other Name': The Issue of Inclusive Language," Field-Bibb insists that the ultimate priority assumed for fatherhood in Ricoeur's "Fatherhood: From Phantasm to Symbol" must be subjected to feminist criticism, but here she also suggests the possibility of constructively using Ricoeur's metaphorical displacement between "is not" and "is" for symbols of God [*The Modern Churchman*, vol. XXXI, no. 2 (1989), pp. 5–9]. Cf. chapter two, "Myth and History: Innocence and Sin" below.

[118] Granted Ricoeur recognizes in symbolism of Adam and Eve, "a very masculine resentment, which serves to justify the state of dependence in which all, or almost all, societies have kept woman" (*The Symbolism of Evil*, pp. 254–55).

[119] Ricoeur, *The Rule of Metaphor: Multi-Disciplinary Studies of the Creation of Meaning in Language* (Toronto: University of Toronto Press, 1977).

[120] Sallie McFague, *Metaphorical Theology* (London: SCM, 1983), pp. 37–40, 65–75, 108, 114.

[121] Ricoeur, "Fatherhood: From Phantasm to Symbol," p. 473.

It was seen, in "A Post-Hegelian Kantian Standpoint" section of this chapter, that a reflexive conception of humanity is constituted by concrete reflection. The reflexive process can now be understood as the continual attempt to recognize the symbols that give rise to genuine human self-understanding.[122] I leave open the question as to how the two-Adams myths could constitute the self-consciousness of "humanity." Yet this process of reflection remains concrete, according to Ricoeur, in that the recognition of the ideal unity of the human project is achieved only by way of the mediation of the signs, symbols, and myths, which constitute authentic works of culture; and these works also evince the possibility of transcending such transience of human culture as social hierarchies. A Hegelian style of concrete reflection provides philosophical instruments, which eventually lead Ricoeur to formulate a post-Kantian hermeneutics of critical thought and restorative criticism. In particular, this concrete process of critical hermeneutics can be reinterpreted with reference to the social and spiritual transformation of human consciousness and circumstances—for women and men—that has as its goal a practical realization of the eschatological kingdom.

The conclusion of this chapter is that the contexts of the construction and reception of Ricoeur's Kantian project have vital philosophical and theological significance. We can also conclude that, in the light of Ricoeur's project, Kant's ideas of reason are not merely illusions which must be tirelessly deconstructed, but unavoidable presuppositions of rational thought and action which must be carefully reconstructed. Recognition of the critical and hermeneutical contexts that inform Ricoeur's position obviously highlights his project as being uniquely restorative of meaning at the same time as it is iconoclastic. It should be emphasized that the cognitive dimension of Ricoeur's ever-developing project is essentially dynamic. We will see in subsequent chapters that narrative refigurations, in particular, become privileged vehicles for a dynamic redescription of the world in which new configurations are unfolded, new forms of knowledge and understanding are constituted. In the next chapter I critically reconstruct Ricoeur's dual-aspect account of human willing. It is my contention that this account can serve, for Ricoeur, as one of the vitally necessary prerequisites in the constitution of

---

[122] Cf. Klemm, *The Hermeneutical Theory of Paul Ricoeur*, pp. 61, 66–73, 106–08.

new formations of knowledge as they might engender new emancipative forms of humanized praxis.[123]

---

[123] On marxist, existentialist, pragmatic, and analytic uses of praxis see Richard Bernstein, *Praxis and Action* (London: Duckworth, 1972), especially pp. 1–9, 13ff, 76–83, 316–18.

2

Ricoeur's Dual-Aspect Account of Human Willing

The second of my general claims is that Ricoeur contributes to both post-Kantian critique and reconstruction or, in the hermeneutical terms discussed at the outset of chapter one, to critical thought and restorative criticism. The present chapter supports this claim with elucidation of Ricoeur's dual-aspect account of human willing. His account is characterized by a human subject who is not merely passive in receiving the intuitions of experience, but is actively involved in the constitution of objective experience and in the self-recognition of human freedom. We will find that Ricoeur's account of willing offers a post-Kantian reconstruction of human freedom, temporality/non-temporality and the mediating archetype of humankind. The problem is that his post-Kantianism reflects dichotomies which have become the object of modern and postmodern critiques. Yet a viable alternative for contemporary thought to any narrowly deconstructive critique[1] can be seen in Ricoeur's hermeneutical practice of restorative criticism.

In this context contemporary refers to thought which has confronted the radical critiques of the western tradition as they have been developed after Marx, Nietzsche, and Freud. Moreover, as suggested in the previous chapter, the three masters of suspicion can be understood as foreshadowed by Kant's critiques concerning knowledge of the self, God, and the end of all things. Kant's account of human experience is privileged precisely because it provides the necessary framework for appreciating the continuing contemporary significance of Ricoeur's philosophy of the will, that is, Ricoeur's account of human freedom and sin, as well as his critique of illusory images of God.

---

[1] For a more helpful discussion of deconstructive practices see, as noted earlier, Christopher Norris, *Deconstruction: Theory and Practice*.

In addition to their philosophical importance Kant's critiques together serve Ricoeur as a model for a critique which does not so much dispute the very possibility of theology as it aims to uncover the ideological or illusory character of specific constructions. This post-Kantian use of critique forces contemporary theology to recognize that its authentic subject matter must be *practical*. Ricoeur is readily aware that a critique of theology after Kant must deconstruct[2] objectifying constructions of pure theoretical reason, especially those of self and God conceived as objects of absolute knowledge. Also, following Kant, Ricoeur recognizes that God can only be understood in the context of the freedom of subjects and so in a context in which reason becomes practical. As a post-Kantian philosopher Ricoeur is, in this way, inevitably led to reconstruct the questions Kant sees as unifying all the interests of reason: 1. What can I know? 2. What ought I to do? 3. What may I hope?[3]

As discussed in the previous chapter Ricoeur's project takes Kant's critique of human knowledge as paradigmatic for a certain deconstruction of the illusory aspects of such constructions as God the Father. Yet the kingdom of God serves as a unifying concept for Ricoeur's dual-aspect account of human willing. The eschatology represented by this concept can become a point of contact for postmodern discussions concerning an endless deferral of meaning and the non-closure of historical narratives. For Ricoeur,

> philosophy discovers… the dependence of the self …on the sacred glimpsed in its eschatology.
> …[This] is indeed the promised land for a philosophy that begins with language and with reflection; but, like Moses, the speaking and reflecting subject can only glimpse this land before dying.[4]

The subtext for the eschatology described above is the Old Testament narrative about Moses. The distinctive point is that Ricoeur does not refer to what might be thought to be the completion of meaning, or the closure of narrative, represented by Christ in the New Testament. The question to be raised is whether or not Ricoeur's critique—his restorative

---

[2] I use this term in Ricoeur's sense of critical analysis of philosophical constructions as distinguished in chapter one footnotes 7 and 108.

[3] Kant, *Critique of Pure Reason* B833; cf. Ricoeur, "Biblical Hermeneutics: The Parables of Jesus," *Semeia*, vol. 4 (1975), pp. 139–45.

[4] Ricoeur, "Existence and Hermeneutics," trans. Kathleen McLaughlin, in *The Conflict of Interpretations*, p. 24.

criticism—of the meaning of theological language fully meets certain of the radical challenges of modern and/or postmodern philosophy.

From the three masters of suspicion I take Nietzsche in this chapter to be typically representative of an intransigent modernist critique of theology. Furthermore this critique is radicalized by such French neo-Nietzscheans as Michel Foucault. In fact Foucault proclaims the "death of man" in Paris at the very same time in the 1960s when Ricoeur announces the urgent need for a philosophical anthropology.[5] The radical challenge confronting Ricoeur's post-Kantian position, then, has a double origin: it comes both from his contemporary Foucault and his predecessor Nietzsche.

Although not his strongest statements, Nietzsche's accusations in *The Genealogy of Morals* regarding the illusory nature of the concepts of the kingdom of God, faith, love, hope have relevance here:

> "And what do they call that which comforts them in all their sufferings—their phantasmagoria of future bliss?"
> "Do I hear correctly? They call it Judgment Day, the coming of *their* kingdom, the 'Kingdom of God.' Meanwhile they live in 'faith,' in 'love,' in 'hope.'"
> ...Faith in what? Love for what? Hope of what? There can be no doubt that these weaklings, too, want a chance to be strong, to have *their* kingdom come. They call it simply the kingdom of God—what admirable humility! But in order to have that experience one must live a very long time, beyond death; one must have eternal life to indemnify oneself for that terrestial life of faith, love and hope.[6]

In part Ricoeur faces Nietzsche's challenge in his contribution, with Alasdair MacIntyre, to *The Religious Significance of Atheism*.[7] His response to Nietzsche is assessed in the third section of the present chapter.

At this point let us return to Kant who provides the background to Ricoeur's hermeneutics of suspicion. In order to recognize his dual-aspect account of the will we need to elucidate those anthropological and theological concepts which are presupposed by Ricoeur's phenomenological analysis of human willing. I will aim to assess critically Ricoeur's concepts of human willing and so uncover any residual transcendental idealism. In its bare essentials, transcendental

---

5 See my "A Question of Personal Identity."

6 Nietzsche, *The Birth of Tragedy and the Genealogy of Morals*, trans. Francis Golffing (Garden City, NY: Double day, 1956), p. 182.

7 Alasdair MacIntyre and Paul Ricoeur, *The Religious Significance of Atheism* (New York: Columbia University Press, 1969).

idealism here is the view which assumes that certain unknowable *a priori* concepts are necessary conditions for the very possibility of human experience.[8]

With regard to Ricoeur's anthropological concepts, as mentioned in chapter one, the will is understood in Kantian terms as a limiting concept.[9] This means that the will serves as a construct which cannot be known in itself. To that extent it limits those sorts of claims to knowledge of human freedom which may be made in Ricoeur's dual-aspect account of willing.

With regard to his theological concepts, Christ is said to be in Kantian terms the entire object of our will.[10] Whereas Kant calls the *entire* object of our will the highest good, Ricoeur claims further that only the ideal divine/human will, i.e. a Christ figure, could ever be imagined to achieve this good. This is the entire object of our will in the sense that it encompasses both virtue and happiness, and so both the rational and sensible aspects of our willing. As Kant says,

> pure reason always...demands the absolute totality of conditions for a given conditioned thing... it follows that an unavoidable illusion arises from the application of the rational idea of the totality of conditions (and thus of the unconditioned) to appearances.
>
> ...reason in its practical employment is not a bit better off. As pure practical reason it likewise seeks the unconditioned... this is sought as the unconditioned totality of the object of the pure practical reason, under the name of the *highest good.*
>
> ...the highest good may be [thought to be] the entire *object* of a pure practical reason, i.e. of a pure will.
>
> ...Inasmuch as virtue and happiness together constitute the possession of the highest good for one person, and happiness in exact proportion to

---

[8] Helpful for what I attempt to establish with reference to Ricoeur's dual-aspect account of human willing is Henry Allison's account of these necessary conditions as "epistemic conditions;" in this light, then for us, the problem—even the unresolved question—is whether or not Ricoeur assumes an *ontological* distinction, i.e. whether the dual-aspects represent two distinct beings or even two conditions of being as in temporal man and eternal God. See Henry Allison, *Kant's Theory of Freedom* (Cambridge: Cambridge University Press, 1990), pp. 3–6, 41–53, 73–76, 138–40; also relevant is Allison, "Transcendental Idealism: The 'Two Aspect' View," in Bernard den Ouden and Marcia Moen (eds), *New Essays on Kant* (New York and Bern: Peter Lang, 1987), pp. 155–78.

[9] Ricoeur, *Freedom and Nature*, p. 169; cf. Kant, *Critique of Pure Reason*, B311–12/A256.

[10] Cf. Kant, *Critique of Practical Reason*, trans. Lewis White Beck (Indianapolis: Bobbs-Merrill, 1956), pp. 111–20.

morality (as the worth of a person and his worthiness to be happy) constitutes that of a possible world, the highest good means the whole, the perfect good.

...Since, however, this combination [of virtue and happiness] is known as *a priori*...not derivable from experience, and since the possibility of the highest good therefore rests on no empirical principles, the deduction of this concept must be transcendental. It is *a priori* necessary to bring forth the highest good through the freedom of the will.[11]

We will read the unconditioned and the conditioned in terms of non-temporality and temporality; also Ricoeur's concept of Christ as the entire object of our will may be supposed as *a priori*, i.e. not derivable from experience. It follows that we can only imagine the figure of Christ as achieving the highest good in a possible world; in fact application of this rational (as well as non-temporal) idea seems to be illustrative of Kant's unavoidable illusion. Again in theological terms this possible world could only be the kingdom of God.

As we will find, Ricoeur offers a theologically significant account of the relationship between temporality and non-temporality. Yet we will have to conclude that this account however interesting does not surpass transcendental idealism. In fact Ricoeur's hermeneutical reconstruction of Kant assumes the unknowable conditions of human experience which characterizes the dual-aspect view of transcendental idealism (noted above); or, in other words, the limited character of self-knowledge serves as the starting point for an indirect strategy of interpretation of signs, symbols, and myths. In summing up, I intend to highlight Ricoeur's less abstract, more socially significant insights.

I. Concepts of the Will

This first section introduces three conceptual issues; their more detailed assessment is provided in the second section below. The issues relate to the will understood as a limiting concept, to Christ conceived as the entire object of our will, and to free will interpreted in terms of contemporary analytic philosophy.

The first issue arises due to the fact that Ricoeur's concept of the will is open to rival Kantian and Husserlian interpretations. In his description of deciding in *Freedom and Nature* Ricoeur proposes that the will is a

---

[11] Ibid., pp. 111, 112, 113, 115, 117.

limit-construction.[12] This limit-construction is described in the moment of consenting as a Kantian idea, that is, as regulative and not constitutive.[13] However Ricoeur claims that the will is also to be seen, in phenomenological terms, as an integrating essence in relation to a whole range of limiting concepts. The will and these other limiting concepts are described as both Kantian regulative ideas and Husserlian ideal essences.

The limiting concepts of human willing have two interpretations: they are the regulative ideas of freedom imagined as not being subject to any natural motivation, incarnate, and contingent; and they are the ideal essences of freedom as perfectly enlightened, gracious, and creative.[14] The common point to be gleaned from this dual interpretation is that Ricoeur's account of human free will—influenced, as it is, by both Kant and Husserl—should be read as presenting a whole range of temporal and non-temporal ideas. These ideas characterize his philosophical anthropology.

In brief Ricoeur's original project describes the will as a unity of the voluntary and the involuntary structures of consciousness. This involves both Kantian and Husserlian elements. On the one hand, the will constitutes a limiting concept in that the reciprocal relation of voluntary and involuntary serves as a regulative rule of unity. This restricts claims to knowledge of a purely free will by interpreting freedom in relation to temporal conditions. On the other hand, the act of willing is also described in terms of the correlative meanings of human consciousness as constituted by the intuition of an ideal essence. The danger, then as seen in the previous chapter, is subjective idealism and solipsism. Although his concept of the will may be interpreted in relation to Husserl as well as to Kant, I stress the influence of Kant.

David Klemm gives a different hermeneutical account.[15] While noting Ricoeur's use of a Kantian limit, Klemm stresses the significance of Husserl and Heidegger for reading Ricoeur's philosophical anthropology. In contrast to Klemm's interpretation, my focus upon Ricoeur's Kantian account raises a crucial question. Ricoeur may introduce Kantian limits into his phenomenological analysis of willing in order to avoid both Hegelian absolute idealism and Husserlian subjective

12 Ricoeur, *Freedom and Nature*, p. 169.
13 Ibid., p. 484; cf. Kant, *Critique of Pure Reason*, A689, A702/B717, B730.
14 Ricoeur, *Freedom and Nature*, pp. 425–27 and 484–86.
15 David Klemm, "The Evolution of Ricoeur's Thought from Reflective Philosophy into a Hermeneutic Phenomenology," in *The Hermeneutical Theory of Paul Ricoeur*, pp. 45–61.

idealism. But does this only lead him to engender another problematical form of idealism?[16]

The second issue of concern is the mediating representation of Christ as the entire object of the human will. As explained above Ricoeur assumes that Christ, as the mediating figure of non-temporality and temporality, represents in Kantian terms the whole, the perfect good which is the entire object of our will.[17]

The above suggests that a transcendental idealist problematic underlies Ricoeur's complex project of an eidetics, an empirics, a hermeneutics, and the still incomplete poetics of the will. The import of his philosophy of the will, as becomes evident at each level of his developing project, depends upon a potentially illusory relation of the temporal and the non-temporal in the act of willing. The eidetic level of description of willing already involves assuming the existence of a bond between the non-temporal ideal of the voluntary and the necessary temporal structures of the involuntary.[18]

To understand the important yet highly questionable problematic it is essential to recognize that Ricoeur's projected poetics of human willing presupposes the functioning of the imagination in its productive schematizing role of representing the rational idea of totality or unity in narrative form. Accepting Ricoeur's presupposition with regard to his poetics, a transcendental idealist problematic is apparent insofar as what must appear a paradoxical unity of the temporal and the non-temporal in the act of willing is ideally represented by the mythico-poetic imagination.[19]

Ricoeur's post-Hegelian Kantianism comes to the surface at this point. As in the previous chapter the temptation of Hegelianism for Ricoeur lies in the demand of reason to seek the totalization of time in non-time. The references to Christ in this chapter suggest that the figure of Christ, or the archetype, represents the rational idea of totality. That is to say the Judaeo-Christian narratives can be easily interpreted in this

---

[16] Ibid, p. 49; and Ricoeur, "Kant and Husserl," in *Husserl: An Analysis of His Phenomenology*, trans. E. Ballard and L. Embree (Evanston: Northwestern University Press, 1967), pp. 175–201.

[17] Ricoeur, "Hermeneutics of Symbols and Philosophical Reflection, I" and "The Demythization of Accusation," trans. Peter McCormick, in *The Conflict of Interpretations*, pp. 310–11 and 344–47; "Biblical Hermeneutics: the Parables of Jesus," p. 145. Cf. Kant, *Critique of Practical Reason*, p. 112ff.

[18] Ricoeur, *Freedom and Nature*, pp. 37–38, 149–63, 425–28.

[19] Ricoeur, "The Demythization of Accusation," *The Conflict of Interpretations*, p. 346.

context to represent the self-temporalizing of God whereby Christ's self-activity constitutes the mediation of the conflict of the voluntary and the involuntary concomitant with the conflict of non-temporality and temporality. The biblical myths of the first and second Adam are, then, made comprehensible for the experience of dual-aspect beings. These become the symbolic representation of both the temporal experience of sin and the non-temporal restoration of innocence.[20]

In essays and works which develop his phenomenology of the will, Ricoeur refers to Christ as the mediating archetype, as the exemplar of the highest good which, again, is the entire object of our will. Yet how, it can be asked, are these references to be understood historically and, as Ricoeur obviously intends, symbolically in the context of the narratives of the origin and the end of evil? There is not a simple answer to this question. Already in his "Objectivity and Subjectivity in History," Ricoeur wants to preserve both the objective truth of human history and various narrative representations of that history.[21] As will be seen in the last section of this chapter, Ricoeur speaks both symbolically and historically about Christ.

Finally, with regard to the third conceptual issue of concern in the present section, it is deemed useful to appropriate certain concepts from contemporary analytic philosophy. I will attempt to contextualize Ricoeur's discussion of freedom and nature for possible critical dialogue with Anglo-American philosophers. Important in interpreting Ricoeur's Kantian references to the will as a limiting concept and to Christ as the entire object of our will are the analytic categories used to assess theories of the will according to the opposed standpoints of compatibilism or incompatibilism.

It is significant to recognize that, if placed in the context of contemporary analytic philosophy, a reading of Ricoeur may suffer a fate similar to a reading of Kant as has been recounted by Allen Wood.[22] Wood recognizes the temptation to read Kant as showing not only the compatibility of freedom and determinism, but also the compatibility of compatibilism and incompatibilism; and the same could be said similarly of Ricoeur's account of freedom and determinism. Yet Wood reconstructs

---

[20]   Ricoeur, *Freedom and Nature*, pp. 33–34; and *The Symbolism of Evil*, pp. 350–57.

[21]   Ricoeur, "Objectivity and Subjectivity in History," pp. 26–27, 31, 38.

[22]   "Kant's Compatibilism," in Allen Wood (ed.), *Self and Nature in Kant's Philosophy* (Ithaca: Cornell University Press, 1984), especially p. 74ff. For a more developed, critical discussion of Wood see Allison, *Kant's Theory of Freedom*, pp. 28, 47–51, 252, 255–56.

Kant's account by categorizing him with compatibilists who hold that human actions may be determined by natural causes and also be free in the sense necessary for moral agency and responsibility. He also admits that Anglo-American commentators have tended to put Kant along with incompatibilists who maintain that if our actions are determined by natural causes, then free agency and moral responsibility are illusions.[23]

Now if the compatibilist interpretation of Ricoeur, as a Kantian, is wrong so too is the incompatibilist. An accurate account of the will as a limiting concept, which can be read as a regulative unity of the voluntary and the involuntary as well as a phenomenological correlation of activity and passivity, would represent human freedom in a mutual relation with a causally determined nature. But, as Ricoeur himself says,

> the determination of choice by clear reason represents an idea which is not derived from experience by abstraction... but which is formed by idealization. It represents a limit-form of freedom, a freedom brought about by a perfectly clear and rational motivation. All equilibrium, all indifference of motives would be excluded from this freedom. Hence the determination of willing would mean that the practical evidence which resides in rational evaluation ipso facto determines the univocity of the imperative of choice. All that...is an ideal standard of human willing, according to which perfection of choice is proportionate to the rationality of motivation ...The only necessity which appears here is not a necessity of a succession of acts, but the necessity of a continuity of contents of intellectual meanings, assuming that we consider them attentively.
>
> ...this limit hypothesis holds considerable interest: it is what permits us to isolate by contrast the genuine indetermination proper to freedom which subsists even though all difference has disappeared from motivation.[24]

This dual-aspect interpretation of the partial determination and relative indetermination of human freedom makes Ricoeur appear, in analytical terms, to be an unconventional compatibilist. Ricoeur supports the controversial dual-aspect interpretation of Kant on free will which is affirmed by philosophical commentators such as Wood but challenged by nineteenth- and twentieth-century philosophers such as Henry

---

[23] Certain recent Kantian commentators have begun to confront the serious difficulty for Kant that freedom (and morality) may be illusory. Notably Onora O'Neill emphasizes this difficulty in her significant review, "Henry Allison, *Kant's Theory of Freedom,*" *Bulletin of the Hegel Society of Great Britain*, double issue, nos 23/24 (1991), pp. 108–11.

[24] Ricoeur, *Freedom and Nature*, pp. 183–84.

Sidgwick, Lewis Beck, and Jonathan Bennett.[25] More detailed critical scrutiny must be applied to this controversial dual-aspect interpretation of Kantian concepts.

II. Freedom, Temporality/Non-temporality, and the Mediating Archetype

In *Freedom and Nature* Ricoeur aims to unite nature and freedom and, in order to do so, he takes up Kant's dual-aspect account of human free will. As suggested above Ricoeur, like Kant, may be understood to be an unconventional compatibilist.[26] His phenomenology of the will begins with the premise that freedom and nature are utterly distinct yet the terms of the voluntary and the involuntary are not found to be unrelated in conscious experience. The detailed phenomenological description of the three moments of deciding, acting, and consenting in *Freedom and Nature* reflects Ricoeur's aim to elucidate thoroughly the reciprocal relation of the voluntary and the involuntary aspects of conscious experience in an act of willing. For Ricoeur, then, the voluntary/involuntary act of the human subject brings together freedom and nature, and so mediates the Kantian conflict between reason and sensibility.

It should be recalled that Kant's overall conception of experience is shaped by two main concerns. First, he aims to limit knowledge claims concerning what human beings experience to what is received and taken up from sensible intuition. Second, Kant intends to ground morality and religion in pure practical reason. This twofold concern to limit the domain of empirical knowledge and to preserve the interests of morality is evident in the way in which the Third Antinomy of Pure Reason in the *Critique of Pure Reason* is restated and resolved in the terms of Kant's *Critique of Practical Reason*.

Allow me to emphasize those points from Kant which become fundamental to Ricoeur's concepts of human freedom and temporality.

---

[25] See Henry Sidgwick, "The Kantian Conception of Free Will," *Mind* XIII (1888), pp. 405–12, reprinted in *Methods of Ethics* (London: Macmillan, 1966); Lewis White Beck, *A Commentary on Kant's Critique of Practical Reason* (Chicago: University of Chicago Press, 1960); Jonathan Bennett, *Kant's Dialectic* (Cambridge: Cambridge University Press, 1974); and Allen Wood, "Kant's Compatibilism," and Jonathan Bennett, "Kant's Theory of Freedom," in Wood (ed.), *Self and Nature in Kant's Philosophy*. Cf. Allison, *Kant's Theory of Freedom*.

[26] Ricoeur, *Freedom and Nature*, pp. 19, 78, 483–85.

To begin with, Kant's resolution in the first *Critique* alone of the antinomy of transcendental freedom and natural necessity depends upon his dual-aspect account of human experience. The crucial distinguishing feature of this account is that a human subject does not merely receive discrete perceptions—as is especially argued to be the case in an atomistic account of experience (notably in the empiricist account presented by David Hume)—but actively synthesizes the manifold of intuitions in conformity with universal rules of unity.

Also important is that Kant's transcendental arguments concerning both theoretical and practical knowledge reveal the role of the subject in the synthetic unity of human experience. His theoretical philosophy assumes a dimension and an activity of the self which are not immediately observable and are only reached by inferring back from what the structure of the subject must be presumed to be for human experience to be what it is. For Kant a certain "transcendental unity of apperception," or connectedness, is a necessary structure for our experience and knowledge of an objective world. In his words,

> There can be no modes of knowledge, no connection or unity of one mode of knowledge with another, without that unity of consciousness which precedes all data of intuitions, and by relation to which representation of objects is alone possible. This pure original unchangeable consciousness I shall name *transcendental apperception.*[27]

> Man, however, who knows all the rest of nature solely through the senses, knows himself also through pure apperception; and this, indeed, in acts and inner determinations which he cannot regard as impressions of the senses. He is thus to himself, on the one hand phenomenon, and on the other hand, in respect of certain faculties the action of which cannot be ascribed to the receptivity of sensibility, a purely intelligible object.[28]

Similarly the morally free subject is not merely dispersed by diverse desires and inclinations, but must recognize himself or herself as the unifying ground behind the maxims of all moral action.[29] Kant's descriptions of the subject's active role in experience involve concepts which are not strictly empirical.[30] In particular we know ourselves to be free *a priori*.[31]

---

[27] Kant, *Critique of Pure Reason*, A107.
[28] Ibid., A546–47/B574–75.
[29] Kant, *Critique of Practical Reason*, p. 122.
[30] Kant, *Critique of Pure Reason*, A2, B2, A3/B7.
[31] Kant, *Critique of Practical Reason*, p. 4.

Roughly, then, Ricoeur accepts that moral experience is conceivable only insofar as the human subject is considered in both its noumenal and phenomenal aspects and so is understood to be free to determine the will directly as pure practical reason. In the third antinomy of the first *Critique* Kant confronts the dilemma that, on the one hand, the human subject is knowable empirically like all other phenomena in nature and so is caught up in a causal nexus. Yet, on the other hand, the subject is transcendentally speaking free, even though like all noumenal conditions and ideas human freedom cannot be known in itself. Kant attempts to resolve this dilemma in terms of pure practical reason by arguing that it is not inconsistent to conceive of both a "causality according to *nature*" and a "causality arising from *freedom*";[32] and it is the latter which he refers to as "a causality of reason."[33] But it is practical and not speculative reason which is considered to be the "cause *producing* actions."[34] Kant equates pure practical reason with our will; and speaks of the causality of our will.[35] He hopes to reconcile freedom and determinism in the second *Critique* by demonstrating that pure practical reason determines the action of our will at the same time as it manifests the autonomy and so the freedom of the will, which acts for the sake of the moral law of our nature as sensible and rational beings.[36] He argues that autonomy is identical with consciousness of the freedom of the will:

> By this freedom the will of a rational being, as belonging to the sensuous world, recognizes itself to be, like all other efficient causes, necessarily subject to the laws of causality, while in practical matters, in its other aspect as a being in itself, it is conscious of its existence as determinable in an intelligible order of things. It is conscious of this not by virtue of a particular intuition of itself but because of certain dynamic laws which determines its causality in the world of sense...if freedom is attributed to us, it transfers us into an intelligible order of things.[37]

However I want to stress that commentators radically disagree on the problems and insights which accompany this account of freedom. References should be made to certain points of disagreement which help

---

[32] Kant, *Critique of Pure Reason*, A532/B560; also A538/B566.

[33] Ibid., A547/B575.

[34] Ibid., A550/B578.

[35] Ibid., A534/B562.

[36] Kant, *The Moral Law: The Groundwork of the Metaphysics of Morals,* trans. John Paton (London: Hutchinson, 1951), pp. 63, 71, 113 [henceforth *Groundwork*]; also Kant, *Critique of Practical Reason*, p. 32ff.

[37] Kant, *Critique of Practical Reason*, p. 43.

to characterize Ricoeur's interpretation of Kant. Notably neither Lewis Beck nor Jonathan Bennett in their respective interpretations of Kant are convinced that his theory of freedom reconciles freedom and determinism. Beck comments that "Kant... does not seem to have felt the paradox in his own views that all his critics and most of his disciples felt."[38] Similarly, as Bennett observes in *Kant's Dialectic*, "one suspects that if Kant has achieved consistency in his reconciling theory, that is only because one half of it has no real content."[39] Also, in his response to Allen Wood in "Kant's Theory of Freedom," Bennett quotes Beck as having questioned whether Kant's theory is about freedom in any ordinary sense.[40] In contrast Ricoeur as well as Bernard Carnois, one of his students, attempt to reconstruct a much more coherent concept of Kantian freedom, no matter how problematical these reconstructions are. Carnois, for instance, asks: "Is Kant's idea of freedom coherent?" He answers by arguing that

> ...the genesis of a concept, and the way in which it is introduced in a doctrine, tells us a great deal about the nature of that concept... Thus we will trace the evolution of Kant's thought; we will fix the circumstances under which the main concepts of freedom appear...the coherence of an idea manifests itself in large part precisely through its striving toward an equilibrium which is always threatened. ...
> By laying out their genealogy, we have been able to observe how all these concepts converge on the notion of the autonomy of the will...
> ...the complexity of Kant's analysis is simply a faithful reflection of the complexity which inheres in the very essence of human freedom.[41]

It is debatable whether or not Carnois succeeds in developing a case for the overall coherence of Kant's account of freedom. As Onora O'Neill persuasively argues, there is no attempt, in Carnois's endeavor to make a coherent doctrine out of Kant's account of freedom, to relate together freedom, reason, and critique.[42] Carnois is correct to recognize that freedom remains fundamental to Kant's whole philosophical enterprise. Yet reason and critique also need to play significant roles in any attempt

---

[38] Lewis Beck, *A Commentary on Kant's Critique of Practical Reason*, p. 192.

[39] Jonathan Bennett, *Kant's Dialectic*, p. 194.

[40] Bennett, "Kant's Theory of Freedom," in *Self and Nature in Kant's Philosophy*, p. 107; cf. Beck, *A Commentary on Kant's Critique of Practical Reason*, p. 188.

[41] Bernard Carnois, *The Coherence of Kant's Doctrine of Freedom*, trans. David Booth (Chicago: University of Chicago Press, 1987), pp. xiv, 122.

[42] See Onora O'Neill's review of Carnois, *Bulletin of the Hegel Society of Great Britain*, no. 15 (spring/summer, 1987), pp. 38–44.

to elucidate the fundamental structure of Kant's problematic.[43] In this context several questions arise. How does Ricoeur reconstruct Kant's concept of human freedom? How does he understand the compatibility—or, to use a term more appropriate to Ricoeur, the relation—of freedom and nature? Does he give an adequate account of freedom's relation to reason and critique?

In *Freedom and Nature*, Ricoeur develops a formal ontology in which "freedom is both activity and receptivity and so constitutes itself in receiving what it does not produce: values, capacities, and sheer nature."[44] Yet this ontology is only possible, as has already been remarked, if the conflicts of reason and sensibility are, according to Ricoeur, covertly reconciled. His eidetic of willing claims to elucidate the essential unity which lies behind the Kantian antinomies. The analysis of the first moment of willing—that of deciding—reveals that behind the contrast between the inclinations of nature and the principle of freedom there appears a fundamental connection in the sphere of motivation. As Ricoeur says,

> *A posteriori* inclination and *a priori* principles must thus share a common appearance as *motives*. The Kantian [contrast] of duty and sensibility on an ethical level presupposes a broader phenomenology of motivation and decision which embraces even the terms of the [contrast].[45]

It is necessary to explain Ricoeur in terms of Husserl. Ricoeur assumes Husserl's distinction between regional and formal ontologies. For Husserl the concepts fundamental to consciousness—including that of freedom—and the concepts fundamental to nature belong to different regions. These different categories of concepts, then, constitute the respective regional ontologies of consciousness and of nature. Yet these regions share concepts with common meanings such as the real and the possible which in turn constitute a formal ontology as "the sum of determinations of the idea of an object of thought in general."[46]

Kant, in contrast, does not delineate the concepts that appear primitive to the region of consciousness. Instead his description of

---

[43] Cf. Onora O'Neill, "Vindicating Reason," in Paul Guyer (ed.), *The Cambridge Companion to Kant* (Cambridge: Cambridge University Press, 1992), pp. 280–308.

[44] Ricoeur, *Freedom and Nature*, p. 484.

[45] Ibid., pp. 130–31.

[46] Ibid.; and Husserl, *Idées directrices pour une phénoménologie, tome premier: Introduction générale à la phénoménologie*, trad. de Paul Ricoeur (Paris: Éditions Gallimard, 1950).

phenomena remains, in Husserl's terminology, under the "natural attitude" (*die naturliche Einstellung*) which concerns itself with the permanent factual yet non-essential conditions of the appearance of an object (or, a mere fact, *Faktum*) in the natural world. Ricoeur uses a version of the phenomenological reduction to bracket this natural attitude in order to discover the essential unity of phenomena in consciousness and, in particular, to make manifest the primitive concept of freedom in the region of consciousness.[47]

However, even after Ricoeur's attempt in his eidetic description to unify the voluntary and the involuntary structures of consciousness, the problem remains that phenomenological analysis of the lived experience of human freedom still has to confront the fundamental paradox which Kant recognized concerning the form of time and its relation to freedom. As Ricoeur says, the form of temporal succession appears to be both "undergone" (*subite*) and "directed" (*conduite*). In terms of Ricoeur's phenomenological analysis the temporal succession of discrete acts is involuntary to the extent that it does not depend on the human subject. Yet description of the sphere of motivation shows that through the choice and project of willing the human subject voluntarily orientates himself or herself within an ordered series of acts.[48]

Recalling our discussion of a limit-construction, we see that such reasoning according to a limit informs Ricoeur's construction of the concept of an only human freedom. To reiterate, his Kantian-derived concept of freedom needs to be understood in relation to the regulative idea of God as absolute freedom with "a simultaneous character of indetermination and self-determination, the limit of a perfectly motivated freedom, the incarnation of a gracious freedom and the utopia or ideal of a necessarily creative freedom."[49] For Ricoeur, human freedom is "an image of the absolute in its indetermination, identical with its power of self-determination but other than the absolute in its reception."[50]

In *Fallible Man*, Ricoeur considers further the idea of human freedom as being both active and passive but, in this context, in relation to an ethical vision of the world. He argues that the antinomy between human freedom and natural causality, which renders impossible any unifying relation of the laws of nature and the responsibility of an ethical subject,

---

[47] Ricoeur, *Freedom and Nature*, pp. 196–97.
[48] Ibid., p. 152.
[49] Ibid., p. 484.
[50] Ibid.

is the result of a complete objectification of the natural world. In other words, "human choice finds itself expelled, exiled from a nature which is entirely reduced to physical causality."[51] Similarly, when Kant's theoretical antinomy of freedom and determinism is put in terms of practical reason, it is recognized to be part of the experience of a rational, embodied being who is free to fulfil the universal law which constitutes the rational aspect of its dual nature. In phenomenological terms the world of the embodied dual-aspect being is "the passive pre-given universal of all judgmental activities."[52] In order to elucidate the antinomic structure of human reasoning itself, that is, of the free act of judgment and the passive aspect of consciousness in its bond with the world, Ricoeur turns to the question of the origin of evil. Evil appears both as an aspect of conscious choice and as an aspect of the universally given. He argues that evil must be understood reciprocally with freedom:

> even if evil were coeval with the root origin of things, it would still be true that it is manifest only in the way it *affects* human existence… evil's place of manifestation is apparent only if it is recognized, and it is recognized only if it is taken up by deliberate choice. The decision to understand evil by freedom is itself an undertaking of freedom which takes evil upon itself.[53]

Ricoeur finds the essence of his ethical vision of the world in Kant's concept of the radical evil, which is recognized when freedom assumes the responsibility for evil and, at the same time, gains a self-understanding. Kant's essay "On the Radical Evil in Human Nature," in *Religion within the Limits of Reason Alone*, connects the formal principle concerning freedom in the second *Critique* and in the *Groundwork to the Metaphysics of Morals* with the problem and origin of evil.[54] However again opinions vary concerning the problems and achievements of Kant's account; in this instance the controversy of opinions concerns the success of his drawing a connection between human freedom and evil.

Carnois presents a comprehensive discussion of this connection between freedom and evil. Possibly due to the practice of assessing together the various contexts of Kant's discussions of free will and not

---

51 Ricoeur, "Philosophy of Will and Action," in *The Philosophy of Paul Ricoeur*, p. 70.
52 Ibid., p. 78.
53 Ricoeur, *Fallible Man*, pp. xxiv–xxv.
54 The present discussion of Kant's moral philosophy and radical evil is based upon Ricoeur's publications prior to *Soi-même comme un autre* (1990). Yet I do refer the reader to a pertinent discussion of Kant in *Soi-même comme autre*, pp. 238–54; *Oneself as Another*, pp. 204–18.

analysing precisely the arguments of specific passages, no insuperable problems emerge in Carnois's account of both freedom and evil.[55] Yet Lewis Beck points out that many defenders of Kant's doctrine of freedom who have accepted the conclusion that a good will is a free will find themselves in a dilemma. That is, if there is evil, it must be a result of a failure to be free.[56] For example, Henry Sidgwick finds an insoluble problem in Kant's doctrine which suggests that only autonomous or moral action actualizes practical freedom. As Sidgwick understands the doctrine, it seems to be that only autonomous action is free, moral action, while heteronomous actions are unfree. The latter category of actions, since being motivated by sensuous desires, must be necessitated by the mechanism of nature. This would imply that no one can be held responsible for heteronomous, immoral actions; a person is, then, only morally responsible for autonomous, moral actions. Yet, as Wood states—and, in my opinion, rightly so—Sidgwick's problem is illusory, because Kant's actual view was that, since the human will is free, heteronomous actions are performed on the basis of sensuous motives without being rationally necessitated by them. Even when human beings act according to sensuous motives they do so with, at the same time, having the capacity to be moved by the *a priori* law of reason. According to Wood humans act as practically free beings and so are responsible.

Beck also addresses Sidgwick's problem by noting that the source of moral responsibility lies in the free act of choice of maxims which, in the essay "On Radical Evil," Kant claims is a choice of a disposition (*Gesinnung*) for either good or evil. Of course fundamental unresolved issues emerge in an exposition of Kant's account of the will's choice of a disposition. For example, John Silber gives a very clear picture of the ethical dynamics of Kant's account of the will. Yet Silber is still forced to ask: Could the will (*Willkür*) freely choose to act according to evil maxims?[57] Or is this grounding of choice only a verbal illusion? Certainly, if there is no human freedom, then for Kant evil does not exist either, since there would only be non-moral animality or natural causation. Returning again to Ricoeur's point of view, it can be asserted that, according to his reconstruction of Kant, the choice of an evil or good disposition as the ultimate subjective ground of all moral maxims is itself the responsibility of a free will.

---

[55] Carnois, *The Coherence of Kant*, pp. 83–109.

[56] Beck, *A Commentary on Kant's Critique of Practical Reason*, p. 203.

[57] Silber, "The Ethical Significance of Kant's *Religion*," in *Religion within the Limits of Reason Alone*, pp. lxxix–cxxxiv.

In sum, Ricoeur's reconstruction of freedom and temporality/non-temporality can be seen in his reference to the noumenal choice of the disposition of the free will whereby "I am constituted as a self over and above all my choices and individual acts."[58] Ricoeur argues that "not only is it true that freedom is the ground of evil, but the avowal of evil is also the condition of the consciousness of freedom."[59] In this avowal there may be detected "the delicate connection of the past and future, of the self and its acts."[60] Ricoeur associates the temporal awareness of human evil with the consciousness of a fault (*une faute* or *une faille*) which he describes as a rift (*un écart*) in the original constitution of human reality. The fault presents structural evidence of a more primordial disposition prior to all moral (evil) acts. For Ricoeur, Kant's recognition of a noumenal disposition over and above all individual acts points to the total and essential unity of a primordial subject. He claims to relate this recognition of an ideal unity to Kant's notion of the noumenal causality of a transcendental subject which must involve the non-temporal affecting the temporal.[61]

But what does it mean to speak of a noumenal causality? Is this not a contradiction in terms, since it is the phenomenal world that is governed by the laws of cause and effect, while the noumenal world is supposed to be the realm of freedom? Equally what can it mean to say that the non-temporal affects the temporal? It is my conclusion that Ricoeur justifies the use of contradictory terms such as noumenal causality and references to non-temporal activity insofar as they reflect the paradoxical nature of the account that must be given of the subject of human freedom as being both active and passive in the constitution of human experience. Of course this justification depends upon accepting Kant's transcendental idealism.[62] This means accepting *both* natural determinism and the kind of freedom necessary for moral agency. Both determinism and freedom are conceivable, according to a certain transcendental idealist interpretation of Kant, insofar as events in time follow a necessary order

---

58 Ricoeur, *Fallible Man*, p. xxvi.
59 Ibid., p. xxviii.
60 Ibid.
61 Kant, *Critique of Pure Reason*, A448–50/B476–78; we might also consider the good will in the *Groundwork*. Cf. *Fallible Man*, p. xxvii; and *Soi-même comme un autre*, pp. 239–54; *Oneself as Another*, pp. 204–18.
62 For critical discussion of Kant's transcendental idealism as it can be read on questions concerning noumenal causality and freedom, on "the air of paradox" surrounding the intelligible and empirical character of rational agency, e.g. "timeless agency," again see Allison, *Kant's Theory of Freedom*, pp. 28–29, 39–52, 140–43.

as determined by their natural causes while, at the same time, a noumenal choice (i.e. a particular non-temporal choice, if this is not a contradiction in terms) affects an empirical character and so determines the moral history of that character. In other words, as seen in the *Religion*, the noumenal choice is a free choice (of a non-temporal being) which decides the disposition of the fundamental maxim on which a temporal being will act.

III. Myth and History: Innocence and Sin

The theological significance of Ricoeur's dual-aspect account of human freedom and temporality becomes increasingly obvious. For instance, according to this account an innocent freedom is ultimately only fully conceivable as non-temporal—i.e. as that of a non-human being. In order to draw out the implications of this point consider the following. First, Ricoeur holds that the disposition towards evil has its ground of possibility in human disproportion. Yet this disposition can only be understood in the light of an original innocence.[63] Evil is both something that affects the innocent subject and a power by which the subject affects itself.

Second, this paradox means that innocent, non-violent power can only be represented by the symbols and myths which the imagination liberates from human experience. Ricoeur's claim, which gives a partial response to the challenge of Nietzsche, is that

> the utopia of a kingdom of God, a city of God, and empire of minds or a kingdom of ends, implies such an imagination of non-violent power. This imagination liberates the essence, and this essence governs all efforts to transform power into an education to freedom.[64]

Third, the global disposition of "fallibility" (*la faillibilité*), which Ricoeur maintains constitutes "the disproportion" (*la disproportion*) of humankind with itself, suggests that evil could have entered the world with man or woman "for he (or she) is the only reality which presents this unstable ontological constitution of being greater and lesser than himself (or herself)."[65] Being greater than itself means that human freedom is an image of the divine in its indetermination and identical to

---

63 Ricoeur, *Fallible Man*, p. 222; and *The Symbolism of Evil*, p. 156.
64 Ricoeur, *Fallible Man*, p. 182.
65 Ibid., p. 4.

the absolute in its power of self-determination. Being lesser than itself means that human freedom, as Ricoeur also states, is other than the divine in its receptivity. In "The Image of God and the Epic of Man," which we discussed in the previous chapter, Ricoeur further explains that the image of God in human beings can be understood only if the will is not merely determined as a slave to (evil) nature—as *un serf arbitre*—but may be conceived as innocent, free, and autonomous. Moreover he argues,

> Mythical language best preserves the revealing power contained within the *imago dei*. It makes manifest the fact that human nature has been degraded not only in the individual, but also in collectivity....
>
>   The imagination, insofar as it has a mythico-poetic function, is also the seat of profound workings which govern the decisive changes in our vision of the world.[66]

The power of the human imagination to generate a mediating representation of an innocent God-man, or an "archetype of the pure moral disposition," is necessary as the ground of hope that human evil (and sin) might be overcome.[67] Such a figure of hope is represented, for Ricoeur, by the second Adam in the myth of salvation. He claims:

> In the introduction [to *Freedom and Nature*] we called attention to the bond between such myths and a properly religious meaning of deliverance, and have shown how they rejoin pure description as illustration or exemplification of the regional ontology of consciousness.[68]

But what about the philosophical implications of Ricoeur's bringing together myths, which portray a human bond with the sacred, and an unfulfilled ontology? Does not the religious meaning of deliverance and the figure of hope represented by the second Adam reflect an idealism which contradicts Ricoeur's attempt to set Kantian limits to Husserl's phenomenology? In the light of his recurring idealist assumptions and discourse, it is possible to ask the additional question concerning the extent to which Nietzsche's thought on the genesis and historical reinterpretation of morality influenced Ricoeur's philosophical anthropology. Ricoeur's discussions in *Fallible Man* on the representation

---

[66] Ricoeur, "The Image of God and the Epic of Man," *History and Truth*, pp. 117, 127.

[67] Kant, *Religion within the Limits of Reason Alone*, p. 54.

[68] Ricoeur, *Freedom and Nature*, p. 186.

and dissimulation of value-intentions recalls Nietzsche.[69] It recalls, especially the passages in *The Genealogy of Morals*, where Nietzsche argues concerning the genesis, meaning, and history of a moral concept.

> There is no set of maxims more important for an historian than this: that the actual causes of a thing's origin and its eventual uses, the manner of its incorporation into a system of purposes, are worlds apart; that everything that exists, no matter what its origin, is periodically reinterpreted by those in power in terms of fresh intentions.
>
> ...the whole history of a thing, an organ, a custom, becomes a continuous *chain* of reinterpretations and rearrangements, which need not be causally connected among themselves, which may simply follow one another... while forms are fluid, their "meaning" is even more so...
>
> I have emphasized this point of historical method all the more strongly because it runs counter to our current instincts and fashions, which would rather come to terms with the absolute haphardness or the mechanistic meaninglessness of event than with the theory of a will to power mirrored in all process.[70]

In the light of Nietzsche's interpretation of the genesis of morality as lying in the will to power, it is important to question whether or not Ricoeur's philosophy of the will deals consistently with Nietzsche's genealogy of moral concepts. [Notice how different from Nietzsche is Carnois in his description of the genesis of a concept in relation to the autonomy of the will.] Ricoeur's argument concerning a hermeneutics of suspicion stresses the fundamental importance of Nietzsche's genealogical critique of morality.[71] However in *Freedom and Nature* Ricoeur criticizes Nietzsche's will to power and distinguishes his own concept of the will.

> Nietzsche embraces under the name of will to power very different aspects of the life of consciousness which are difficult to distinguish. Within it we can recognize, for one, a power of practical affirmation and self-determination which in the present work we shall develop as will strictly speaking (deciding, moving, consenting), and also a complication of the will in passion and of vitality in the sense of passions of power... The truth is that the Nietzschean analysis cannot be superimposed on our pattern of the voluntary and involuntary. It excludes the distinction between the will and organic life which is the cornerstone of our structure of motivation, and it

---

[69] Ricoeur, *Fallible Man*, pp. 132–40.

[70] Nietzsche, *The Genealogy of Morals*, pp. 209–11.

[71] Ricoeur, *The Religious Significance of Atheism*, pp. 61–87; and *Freud and Philosophy*, pp. 25–26, 32–35, 490.

ignores the problem of the fault which is basic to our theory of passions. In our language the will to power is at the same time will, organic life and passion. If, however, we distinguish the will, as the power of valuating, organic life, and the "bad infinite" of passions of violence and war, do there remain tendencies on the organic level which cannot be reduced to the quest for pleasure and avoidance of suffering? Does there remain an "irascible," a basic appetite for the difficult?

...Precisely in the irascible these passions find a point of least resistance, a temptation which the fascinated consciousness realizes in the fault.[72]

This criticism of Nietzsche's analysis of the will to power confirms that Ricoeur's conception of the will as a duality remains Kantian, i.e. transcendental idealist. Whereas Nietzsche's account of willing excludes the distinction between the free will and organic life, which is central to Kant, Ricoeur retains a dual-aspect account of the relationship between the voluntary and the involuntary structures of human willing. And this account becomes theologically significant for the question concerning the Kantian ideal of the pure moral disposition or, it can be said in this context, the ideal of the dual-aspect being. For Ricoeur, it is Christ who must be recognized as representing the entire object of our will. It is, then, only by accepting the Christ figure as the ideal—as he who portrays the harmonious connection of the involuntary desire for pleasure and the practical imperative of reason (i.e. moral virtue)—that humankind is able to confront existence as faulted. Thus conceived, Ricoeur's view is diametrically opposed to Nietzsche's, since Nietzsche develops an intransigent genealogical critique of idealist conceptions of morality and christology.

It is still difficult in turning to the question of Ricoeur's conception of Christ, as the archetype of humankind, to define the relationship between the archetype and the Jesus of history. Ricoeur's writings on history have continued to develop from the essays in *History and Truth* through to *Time and Narrative*. Yet we must object to the claim of J. Hillis Miller that these recent volumes manifest a literal interpretation of historical, literary, and philosophical texts.[73] Ricoeur's various possible views on the historical Jesus and the connection with Christ as the exemplar of the highest good have to be assessed in relation to the complex ever-increasing corpus of his intellectual work. Especially important in this regard are his lecture "The Contribution of French

---

[72] Ricoeur, *Freedom and Nature*, p. 117.

[73] J. Hillis Miller, "But Are Things As We Think They Are?" *The Times Literary Supplement* (9 October 1987), pp. 1104–1105.

Historiography to the Theory of History," his essay "Myth and History," and his recent "Interpretative Narrative."[74]

In the first of these pieces of work, Ricoeur claims that belonging to a plot is what defines an event as historical. Christ's historicity is recognized in the plots[75] of the narratives about his life, death, and resurrection, that is in configurations which unify the diversity of discrete temporal experiences. In "Interpretative Narrative," Ricoeur explains that the passion narratives bring together the inevitability of a divine plan and the refractory nature of human contingency. In this context Ricoeur sees the christological *kerygma* (i.e. the Christ of faith) being identified with the narrative identity of the Jesus (i.e. the Jesus of history). He says,

> If the narrative mediation characteristic of the gospel in general and of each gospel in particular prolongs the Hebraic theologoumen of a divine plan carried through in spite of... or thanks to... our human refractory nature, and if, furthermore, this mediation specifies the theological project as a christological one, we may ask in the third place [if] there is not something in the christological kerygma that calls for narrative, in an absolutely specific way. ...The equation we are seeking to reconstruct between a narrativized kerygma and a kerygmatized narrative seems indeed to have its rationale in the identity proclaimed between the Christ of faith and the Jesus of history...
>
> It is one of the functions of the narrative art, through the combined interplay of plot and character development, to answer the question of "who?" by indicating what we may call the narrative identity of the character, that is the identity produced by the narrative itself. ...it is a fact that the identity of Jesus remains an acute question throughout the gospels. And...it is perhaps the function of some narratives to deepen the enigma of the character, while clarifying the arrangement of the plot. This identity of Jesus is essential to the equation between the Jesus of history and the Christ of faith. To say who Jesus is, is also to say who the Christ is. And this is what the gospels do, especially the passion narratives.[76]

---

74 Ricoeur, "The Contribution of French Historiography to the Theory of History," the 1978–79 Zaharoff Lecture (Oxford: Clarendon Press, 1980); "Myth and History," in Mircea Eliade (ed.), *Encyclopedia of Religion*, vol. 10 (New York: Macmillan, 1987), pp. 273–81; and "Interpretative Narrative," *The Book and the Text*, pp. 237–57.

75 Also see Ricoeur, "Biblical Hermeneutics," pp. 97–98; "Naming God," *Union Seminary Quarterly Review*, vol. 34, no. 4 (1979), pp. 223–26; *Time and Narrative* I, pp. 56, 65–68, 169–74; and *Time and Narrative* II, p. 8ff.

76 Ricoeur, "Interpretative Narrative," pp. 240–41.

While the narrated events about Jesus are defined as historical in the
light of different plots, the passion of Christ remains without change of
plot. Plots represent the varying ways in which the narrative accounts
concerning Jesus' life, death, and resurrection bring together the different
characters and various events. In turn the unity constituted by the
different historical narratives points to the totality represented by the one
timeless Christ myth.

Although contemporary theologians tend to use myth to refer to a
story whose truth content lies at an other than literal level, Ricoeur, for
his part, implies something more. That more is, I maintain, intimately
related to his dual-aspect account of human experience. For while both
mythical and historical narratives are constituted by emplotment, only
the myth of Christ represents the dual-aspect figure which fully
embodies the non-temporal ideal. In "Myth and History," the remaining
essay referred to above, Ricoeur contends that the mythologization of
history and the historicization of myth should receive equal
recognition.[77] The mythologization of the historical account of Christ's
life is comprehensible as the opposite process to the historicization of the
myth of the first Adam in relation to the second Adam. This hermeneutic
process makes possible the representation of the fundamental dual-
aspects of human self-understanding as mediated through history. It
must be emphasized that although the myth of the second Adam is to
make sense of the meaning of humankind's fundamental bond with the
sacred—a bond which is invariant with reference to history—Ricoeur's
account would not make sense theologically unless he believed that Jesus
Christ as the second Adam represented an actual historical individual.

My reading of Ricoeur's representation of Christ is partially informed
by his later writings on history, although for the most part it is guided by
his account of the mediating archetype of humankind in *Freedom and
Nature*, *Fallible Man*, *The Symbolism of Evil*, as well as by the essays which
restate ideas from these works.[78] It must be granted that Ricoeur gives
various Kantian references to Christ in his early works which
undoubtedly remain obscure without consideration of a wider corpus of
works. For instance, Ricoeur's references to "the ideal exemplar of the
highest good" (*un exemplaire idéal du souverain bien*), "the schematization
of the good principle" (*le schématisme du Bon Principe*) and "the ideal of
the pure moral disposition" (*l'Idéale de la constitution morale pure de*

---

[77] Ricoeur, "Myth and History," p. 281.

[78] Cf. Ricoeur, *Husserl*; *The Conflict of Interpretations*; and *The Philosophy of Paul
Ricoeur*.

l'homme) do appear *prima facie* strange.[79] It is for this reason that we seek to understand them in the light of Kant's schematism of the a priori pure imagination (*reinen Einbildungskraft*), which somehow mysteriously brings together the particular and the universal, and in the light of Ricoeur's hermeneutics of religious signs, symbols, and narratives.

Narratives, especially, often function precariously in both Kant's and Ricoeur's attempts to portray the relationship between the particular and the universal. First, in Kant, if we think of the *Groundwork*, his narrative examples are notoriously difficult to interpret. Kant himself says,

> What is more, we cannot do morality a worse service than by seeking to derive it from examples. ...Even the Holy One of the gospel must first be compared with our ideal of moral perfection before we can recognize him to be such. He also says of himself: "Why callest thou me (whom thou seest) good? There is none good (the archetype of the good) but one, that is, God (whom thou seest not)". But where do we get the concept of God as the highest good? Solely from the Idea of moral perfection, which reason traces *a priori* and conjoins inseparably with the concept of free will. ...[examples] make perceptible what the practical law expresses more generally.[80]

From this we might in fact conclude that, for instance, Kant's *Groundwork* narrative concerning the man who makes promises intending not to keep them is undecidable meaning. Conversely Kant is often interpreted as providing, in the *Groundwork*, the rules whereby one can be certain to act ethically. This would mean that he introduces the narrative about promise-keeping as a bridge between the law as such and any particular norm applied in a specific religious, social, or historical sphere of action. The issue, then, is whether the narrative defines morality as grounded in the universal law or as determined by an example of an ungrounded act. Supposedly such an act would define morality as a linguistic performative to be judged only by an internal temporal consistency which the narrative-example shows.

Second, consider how narrative functions precariously in Ricoeur. As already suggested interpretation of the gospel narratives is assumed to involve recognition of Christ as the ideal of a dual-aspect being. This means that the universal ideal, or archetype, of the highest good is instantiated in a particular human being. But this remains questionable— is this what Kant would call an avoidable illusion? Does Christ depict the possible regeneration of vain, finite quests of faulted existence? In *Fallible*

---

79   Ricoeur, "Freedom in the Light of Hope." See page 31 above.
80   Kant, *Groundwork*, sections 408–9.

Man particular human quests are vain as a consequence of the fault. As was stated earlier, surely Christ could only be imagined as achieving the highest good in a possible world. Perhaps this is why Ricoeur identifies Christ as a figure of hope.[81]

In *Fallible Man*, in contrast with this figure of hope, Ricoeur's anthropology characterizes the dual nature of human existence as fragile. He asserts the disproportion of man or woman with himself or herself [if we assume *l'homme* is a generic term]. Implied in disproportion is the fallibility which constitutes the possibility of evil in human experience. Here awareness of disproportion, fallibility, and evil is manifest in a pre-philosophical language of myth and, especially, in universal symbols of "downfall" (*le déchéance*) and of "guilt" (*la culpabilité*).

Now if the figure of Christ presents symbolically the perfect mediation of the finite and infinite structures which constitute the authentic human quest for the self, then it seems that Ricoeur, as a French Protestant Christian, is assuming a conception of Christ as being uniquely and exclusively the essential mediator between God and humankind.[82] In addition, it might be noted that the essential differences between Protestant interpretations of Christ as the exclusive and unique mediator between God and humankind depend upon the theologian's implicit or explicit philosophical anthropology in the context of which the concepts of human freedom, sin, and grace are criticizable and possibly even revisable.

One possible misconception of Ricoeur's understanding of the relation between concept and symbol might be mentioned. Ricoeur claims that the primary language of symbol "gives rise to [conceptual] thinking" (*donne à penser*).[83] In this regard Sallie McFague argues that the theological significance of Ricoeur's work on metaphor—which follows from and develops his study of symbols—resides in his description of the metaphorical process which constitutes the translation of the symbolic language of human experience (of fallibility and evil) into the conceptual language of theology.[84] Certainly McFague recognizes the relevance of Ricoeur's redescription and translation of the symbolic awareness of the dialectical relationship between the human and the divine into theological concepts. However she reduces the meaning of Ricoeur's use

---

[81] Ricoeur, "Freedom in the Light of Hope," p. 424n.

[82] Ricoeur, *Fallible Man*, pp. 169, 195–96.

[83] Ricoeur appropriates the phrase from Kant, *Critique of Judgement*, trans. J. C. Meredith (Oxford: Clarendon Press, 1952), section 49.

[84] Sallie McFague, *Metaphorical Theology*, pp. 110, 119–22, 213n23, n25.

of metaphor to a comparison, between the affirmative and negative predications "is" and "is not," which is supposed to preserve the tension between the metaphorical and the literal. If through the metaphorical process the symbolic awareness of the sacred is translated into the conceptual thinking concerning God it must, for Ricoeur, involve more than a tension and comparison between the literal and metaphorical.

My contention is that Ricoeur's awareness of the multivalency and ambiguity of symbols (and metaphors) necessitates coming to grips with the source of the open texture and essential incompleteness of the linguistic expressions which arises from the human experiences of disproportion, fallibility, and evil.[85] Again Kant points to the connection of mythical language and philosophical discourse. This connection is crucial for Ricoeur's philosophical anthropology, especially for understanding the diverse actuality of human relationships to the divine. Crucial is Ricoeur's interpretation of the passages in the *Critique of Pure Reason* concerning the mysterious power of the transcendental imagination. As Ricoeur explains in an essay that outlines the framework of *Fallible Man*:

> The first thing one notices in man [or woman] is the two poles: thinking, sensing... I understand what is meant by receiving, being affected; I understand what is meant by intellectual determination. But...their common root, which constitutes precisely the humanity of man [or woman], is "unknown to us"... There is something like a blind spot at the center of a luminous vision, "a blind but indispensable function of the soul."[86]
>
> ...if one calls this synthesis of the understanding and sensibility in the transcendental imagination "consciousness," this consciousness is not yet self-consciousness...
>
> ...A reflection on the "intermediary" role of imagination in the constitution of man [or woman] in his [or her] intimate unity outlines the empty framework within which we must now trace the figure of concrete man [or woman].[87]

It is the discovery of a blind spot at the center of a luminous vision[88] which has to be accounted for in any attempt to trace the figure of concrete man or woman. The difficulty with Ricoeur's attempt to trace

---

[85] Ricoeur, *Fallible Man*, p. 222f.

[86] Kant, *Critique of Pure Reason*, A78.

[87] Ricoeur, "The Antinomy of Human Reality and the Problems of Philosophical Anthropology," pp. 26–27.

[88] Cf. Paul de Man, *Blindness and Insight: Essays in the Rhetoric of Contemporary Criticism* (London: Methuen, 1983).

this figure by way of the intermediary role of the imagination is that he both conceives Christ as the ideal figure of a mythical narrative and considers Jesus as the historical individual of factual or commonsensical historical narratives. To state more precisely this difficulty: the unresolved and, indeed, in principle unresolvable problem for Christian theology remains the nature of human temporality as reflected in the paradoxical figure of Jesus Christ.

William Placher, whose interpretation of Ricoeur is questioned in the previous chapter, draws attention to this unresolvable problem which, he claims, puzzles the biblical interpreter. Ricoeur maintains in different contexts *prima facie* contradictory views regarding his interpretation of Jesus Christ. For instance, it may be, in one context, that the symbol of Christ generates thought whereby meaning is more important than historicity. Equally, in another context, it may be that a symbolic interpretation of Christ is wrong since it loses sight of his historical particularity.[89] However my position is that the deleterious implications of such apparently contradictory propositions notwithstanding, the figure of Christ which, for Ricoeur, symbolically holds together the temporal and the non-temporal aspects of experience, still remains of fundamental significance. Ironically, not only in spite of but also because of the tensions inherent in this duality of time and non-time, the Christian understanding of human history finds its perennial—and, for many, convincing—expression precisely in those biblical narratives which can most easily be read as accounts of humankind's attempts at self-interpretation as a dual-aspect being.

At this juncture let us return to the Kantian background for understanding Ricoeur's account of sin. In order to appreciate fully and to assess critically Ricoeur's symbolism of an evil will, as well as his critique of the concept of original sin, we must keep in mind his dual-aspect account of human free will. Remember that the unconditioned freedom, which somehow constitutes the noumenal choice of acting either according to rational or sensible maxims, is really quite mysterious, since this choice could not be made in time. To explain, this depends upon Kant's doctrine, as set out in the *Religion*, not being primarily concerned with the possibility of a purely rational being, but with a conception of human willing which includes both legislative reason (*Wille*) and the faculty of desire (*Willkür*). *Willkür* is the power of choosing between alternatives; it is determined by an incentive only to

[89] William Placher, "Paul Ricoeur and Postliberal Theology: A Conflict of Interpretations," pp. 44–45.

the extent that the individual has incorporated that incentive into his or her maxim.[90] *Wille* is the purely rational structure which introduces the moral law into the expression of human willing; it does not act temporally. *Wille* in relation to *Willkür* constitutes what the *Religion* calls the predisposition to personality, which is "the capacity for respect for the moral law as *in itself a sufficient incentive of the will (Willkür)*."[91] In a certain sense, then, the moral law determines the freedom of the human subject, but it does not predetermine actions by constituting their grounds in antecedent time. Rather there is a self-determination that signifies a non-temporal mode of causality whereby freedom determines itself.

It is my view that Kant—at least as reconstructed by Ricoeur—is an unconventional compatibilist. Ricoeur's Kantian dual-aspect account of human willing preserves two conflicting claims: that (noumenal) freedom is compatible with (phenomenal) determinism and that freedom is incompatible with absolute determinism. In the *Religion* Kant clearly states that human freedom is incompatible with predeterminism yet compatible with the absolutely spontaneous determination of effects by a self.[92] It is crucial for Ricoeur that Kant, in the *Religion*, also provides the necessary conceptual framework for distinguishing the dual aspects of the temporal and the non-temporal in the freedom of human willing. Evil is then shown to be due to the choice of a maxim which the free will puts forward. Evil does not reside in sensibility nor in the temporal as such; neither is evil the subversion of reason or of the non-temporal. Instead Kant demonstrates that evil is the subordination of moral maxims to sensible maxims. On this Kantian basis Ricoeur is able to claim that "evil is not a something but the subversion of a relation."[93]

It is only with reference to this Kantian conceptual framework that Ricoeur's paradoxical concept of the "servile will" (*le serf arbitre*) in *The Symbolism of Evil* may be properly understood. Kant's framework elaborates the dynamic aspects of *Wille*, *Willkür*, and the *Gesinnung*. In addition, Ricoeur's concept of an "captive free will" (*un libre arbitre captif*) can only be represented by way of the symbolism of evil, since it involves the two contradictory terms of freedom and captivity. Ricoeur proposes that this paradox of a servile will provides the ground for critically

---

90 Kant, *Religion within the Limits of Reason Alone*, p. 19.
91 Ibid., pp. 22–23.
92 Ibid., p. 45n.
93 Ricoeur, "The Hermeneutics of Symbols and Philosophical Reflection, I," trans. Denis Savage, in *The Conflict of Interpretations*, p. 303.

assessing the philosophical problem of evil and, concomitantly, for symbolically reconstructing a contemporary account of sin. He argues that

> evil is a kind of involuntariness at the very heart of the voluntary, no longer over against it but in it and there you have the servile will. ...if evil is at the radical level of "generation"—in a symbolic, not a factual, sense —conversion itself is "regeneration." Thus is constituted, by means of an absurd concept, an *anti-type of regeneration*; because of this anti-type, will is shown to be affected by a passive constitution implied in its actual power of deliberation and of choice.
>
> It is this anti-type of regeneration that Kant tried to elaborate as an *a priori* of the moral life. The philosophical interest of the essay "On Radical Evil"...lies in its having achieved what I a moment ago called the critique of "original sin" as false knowing and in having attempted its "deduction"—in the sense in which the transcendental deduction of the categories is a justification of rules by their power to constitute a domain of objectivity. The evil of nature is thus understood as the condition of possibility of evil maxims, as their ground.[94]

By considering the anti-type of regeneration Ricoeur identifies the Kantian *a priori* ground of the experience of obligation. That is what "ought to be"—i.e. freedom and innocence—"is not." Together the type and anti-type, then, provide the symbolic representation for grasping that evil, although generated by humankind, is not original. Instead evil is a kind of "involuntariness" (*Unfreiwilligkeitheit*) by which the (innocent free) will is enslaved. In phenomenological terms the will is affected by a passive constitution. In other words the will is in a spatio-temporal sense determined by what it receives from nature, i.e. an "inscrutable" (*unerforschbar*) propensity to evil; at the same time the original innocence of the free will is the condition for regeneration.

The question of the origin of evil cannot be avoided in this context. How can an all-powerful holy creator God exist along with the radical evil in human nature? Even if evil is not created by God, how can God's goodness be reconciled with a natural propensity to evil? Ricoeur's reflection on the Book of Job refers to "the death of the god of Providence."[95] What amounts to Ricoeur's critique of the providential God implies an argument for the impossibility of believing in a God who is directly involved in the determination of everything that happens in the world. For Ricoeur, following Kant, a fully autonomous free will

---

94 Ibid., pp. 306–7.
95 Ricoeur, "Religion, Atheism and Faith," p. 455.

must be independent of all outside determination—even of God's will—in order to fulfil the moral law of its own nature. But, if this is so, then is not God breaking the moral law by acting graciously toward humankind and, in Ricoeur's terms, providing the gift of regeneration in the form of his son Jesus Christ? Along with Ricoeur's critique of a providential God goes a claim for the restoration of the meaning of "God." This implies that the religious believer, if not the philosopher of religion, can speak of another "God who would not protect me but would surrender me to the dangers of a life worthy of being called human."[96] Ricoeur concludes that "An idol must die so that a symbol of being may begin to speak."[97]

A concern of the next chapter will be to use Ricoeur's symbolism to answer questions related to the antinomy of grace and freedom. That is, if humankind freely chooses good maxims and strives for the highest good, Why is a gift of regeneration necessary? Or, if there is a radical evil, why assume there is an original free state of innocence? Ricoeur's answer presupposes a certain transcendental deduction of symbols:

> if I use the symbols of deviation, wandering, and captivity as a detector of reality, if I decipher humankind on the basis of the mythical symbols of chaos, mixture and fall, in short, if I elaborate an empirics of the servile will under the guidance of a mythology of evil existence, then I can say that in return I have "deduced"—in the transcendental meaning of the word—the symbolism of human evil. In fact, the symbol, used as a means of detecting and deciphering human reality, will have been verified by its power to raise up, to illuminate, to give order to that region of human experience, that region of confession, which we were too ready to reduce to error, habit, emotion, passivity—in short, to one or another of the dimensions of finitude that have no need of the symbols of evil to open them up and discover them... But the expression, "transcendental deduction of symbols," is not absolutely satisfactory; it orientates us towards the idea that the justification of the symbol of its power to reveal constitutes a simple augmentation of self-awareness, a simple extension of reflexive circumscription, whereas a philosophy instructed by the symbols has for its task a qualitative transformation of reflexive consciousness. Every symbol is finally a hierophany, a manifestation of the bond between humankind and the sacred. Now in treating the symbol as a simple revealer of self-awareness, we cut it off from its ontological function; we pretend to believe that "know

---

thyself" is purely reflexive, whereas it is first of all an appeal by which each man [and woman] is invited to situate himself [or herself] better in being.[98]

For Ricoeur a symbol possesses a double intentionality as a hybrid signifying form composed of both a "literal" and a latent meaning. On the one hand, symbol's intentionality constitutes a level of meaning which, as the term implies, can be distinguished from the metaphorical level of meaning, even if in fact there is no absolute literalness. On the other hand, symbol's latent intentionality refers to the surplus of meaning which makes it possible for Ricoeur to claim that "the symbol gives rise to thought."[99] *The Symbolism of Evil* defines the primary symbols of defilement, sin, and guilt (these will be elaborated the next chapter). These isolatable primary symbols are also woven into myths which, in turn, are characterized as second-degree symbols.

Ricoeur identifies four typical myths each of which in its own unique manner reflects the twofold intentionality of these primary symbols; yet each myth represents a different possible origin of evil. The first three types of myth are distinguished by the way in which each narrative represents, according to its respective set of intentions, an original chaos, mixture, and innocence. Three examples of these types of myth are the great creation epic of *Enuma elish*, the tragic myth represented by *Prometheus Bound*, and the Adamic myth found in *Genesis*. The fourth mythical type is distinguished from the other three as being slightly later; and it is unique in dividing humankind into a soul and a body. The example for this type is the archaic Orphic myth of the exiled soul which represents the soul as divine in its origin but imprisoned in the body. While Ricoeur contends that each of these mythical types is unique his dynamics of the myths intends to demonstrate that the will's original state of being must be that of innocence.[100] So it is that Ricoeur privileges the *Genesis* myth. This myth is privileged because it represents evil as a mode of freedom, while defilement, sin, and guilt are part of human self-consciousness; also the latent meaning of its primary symbols gives rise to thought concerning an original bond with the sacred. Yet as quoted earlier this ontological dependence of the self on the sacred presupposes an eschatology.

We might understand this original bond with the sacred as the symbolic awareness of a fundamental relationship of the temporal and

---

[98] Ricoeur, *The Symbolism of Evil*, pp. 335–36.
[99] Ibid., p. 348.
[100] Ibid., pp. 306–46.

the non-temporal. This remains central to Ricoeur's post-Kantian understanding of moral and religious experience. Together the myths of the first and second Adam represent the archetype of righteousness and the state of innocence as being necessarily prior to the generation of evil but it is also beyond. This state of innocence is imagined or believed to be a non-temporal reality which is both ontological and eschatological. This relationship between the non-temporal conditions for the possibility of freedom and actual temporal experience of evil means that Ricoeur presupposes a transcendental idealist conception, however problematical it may be, of human experience.

In sum, Ricoeur's transcendental idealism is not only a problem for analytical philosophers who are realists but the dichotomies and oppositions which characterize this conception of human experience are precisely the object of postmodern critiques. The binary oppositions between the temporal and the non-temporal, nature and freedom, desire and reason, sin and innocence, human and divine would be brought into question by a deconstructive reading of Ricoeur's text. In fact we might wonder, especially in the light of Nietzsche, how "the non-temporal" can be anything but a mystifying reference! Yet I must admit that Ricoeur's dual-aspect account of human experience results in the significant theological claim that the predisposition towards goodness and the state of innocence, which is to be restored in regeneration, is more original than sin (see chapter three).

IV. The Ideal Exemplar of the Highest Good

From the preceding sections it can be concluded that Kant's antinomy of freedom and determinism as presented in the first and second *Critiques*, as well as his theological antinomy of grace and freedom as it appears in the *Religion*, do not create insoluble problems for either morality or theology. For Ricoeur these conflicts of reason only demonstrate the fundamental limitation of the human will and the necessity of representing symbolically the ideal exemplar of the highest good.

As seen above Ricoeur's symbolism concerning Christ as the ideal exemplar and the archetype depends upon Kant's second *Critique*, *Groundwork*, and *Religion*. Equally the definition from the first *Critique* that a schema provides a rule for the application of universal (and as such non-temporal) concepts to particular instances in time is presupposed by Ricoeur's reference to the schematization of the good principle in Christ.[101] For Ricoeur it seems to follow that the schematization of the good principle constitutes a rule for the universal procedure of the *a priori* imagination to mediate the distance between human evil acts and the good will in the unifying representation of an archetype of humankind. In this light the archetype of Christ is understood as providing a rule for picking out instances of universal goodness as the ideal of human fulfilment. These would be instances of what may be thought to represent the instantiation of the non-temporal in time.

To be more precise about Ricoeur's own account let us consider a rather long and complicated footnote which appears at the end of "Freedom in the Light of Hope." The content of this statement has particular relevance for the central claim of this chapter. Certain of the possibilities and problems encountered in attempting to reconstruct his Kantian concepts concerning the human will, temporality/non-temporality and the mediating archetype appear here. Ricoeur summarizes his interest in Kant's references to the symbolic representation of Christ as follows:

> A historical study of *Religion within the Limits of Reason Alone* should be dedicated to showing just how far the philosopher can go in the representation of the origin of regeneration. The Kantian schematism offers us an ultimate resource here. What we can conceive abstractly as the "good principle," which struggles within us with the "evil principle," we can also represent concretely as the man, pleasing to God, who suffers for the sake of the promotion of the universal good. To be sure, Kant is in no way interested in the historicity of Christ: "this man, the only one pleasing to God," is an Idea. However, this archetype is not at all an idea that I can give myself arbitrarily. Although it is reducible as an event of salvation, this archetype is irreducible as an Idea to a moral intention: "we are not authors of it" (p. 54). It "has established itself in [humankind] without our comprehending how human nature could have been capable of receiving it" (*Ibid.*) That is the irreducible element: "the incomprehensibility of a union between (the good principle) and [human being's] sensible nature" in the moral constitution of humankind (p. 77). Now this Idea corresponds completely with the synthesis demanded by pure reason or, more exactly, with the transcendent object which causes that synthesis. This is not only an example of duty, in which case it would not exceed the Analytic, but an ideal exemplar of the highest good, in that this Idea illustrates the resolution of the Dialectic. Christ is an archetype and not a simple example of duty

---

[101] Ricoeur, "Freedom in the Light of Hope," p. 424; cf. "The Antinomy of Human Reality and the Problems of Philosophical Anthropology," pp. 25–27, 50–57.

because he symbolizes this fulfilment. He is the figure of the End. As such, this "representation" of the good principle does not have for its effect "to extend our knowledge beyond the world of sense but only to make clear *for practical use* the conception of what is for us unfathomable." "Such is the *schematism of analogy*, with which (as a means of explanation)," says Kant, "we cannot dispense" (p. 58n). It is within the strict limits of a theory of the schema and analogy, hence of a theory of transcendental imagination, that the philosopher approaches not only the meanings of hope but the figure of Christ in which the meanings are concentrated.[102]

In the light of this summary by Ricoeur himself it is possible to answer a question raised above. Ricoeur, like Kant, is concerned about the practical usefulness of the schematization of non-temporal concepts; but, unlike Kant, he is also interested in the historicity of Christ. As will be shown in the next chapter, Ricoeur identifies Christ with various titles, each with its own place in a historical understanding of humankind, such as the Son of Man, the second Adam, the Son of God, and the Saviour of sinners.[103]

Before concluding this chapter let us remember a crucial aim in reconstructing Ricoeur's dual-aspect account of human willing. That aim was to assess the extent to which he has confronted the radical critiques of contemporary thought. I turn to this assessment.

To be consistent with the post-Kantian critique of illusory theoretical constructions, I would maintain that Ricoeur's cognitive project of criticism and restoration needs to be directed towards socially meaningful dimensions of human praxis. It should be recognized that his mythico-poetic reconstruction of experience, in narrative form, constitutes not only an intelligible whole out of the heterogeneity of human experience but a communal work and a dynamic praxis. This is to say attention needs to be turned away from the more questionable— mystifying, since philosophically unresolved question of being(s)— elements of Ricoeur's residual idealism in order to focus upon his

---

[102] Ibid.; references in brackets are to the Theodore Greene and Hoyt Hudson translation of Kant's *Religion*.

[103] Ricoeur, *The Symbolism of Evil*, pp. 261–78; *The Conflict of Interpretations*, pp. 45–48, 59–60. By way of a critical note, Ricoeur's exclusive reading of human history according to these patriarchal figures means *l'homme* could not be understood in a generic sense; feminist anthropology would have to reject this reading. At least in his early work Ricoeur tends to privilege traditional western conceptions of religion, culture, race and gender.

socially significant insight concerning *mimesis* and *mythos*.[104] His articulation of *mimesis,* or the representative power of the imagination, and *mythos,* or the narrative emplotment of myth, can be fruitfully contrasted with more radical contemporary French theorists.

Roughly Ricoeur's divergence from his own intellectual milieu can be recognized in the following list of contrasting French modern and postmodern thinkers. To begin with, although Jean-Paul Sartre was persuasive in convincing many of his contemporaries that narrative is the casting of life in the form of an obituary, Ricoeur is still able to claim that narrative is the mode of our living in the world.[105] Also precisely where Roland Barthes perceives the inertia of *doxa* in myths Ricoeur perceives active practical knowledge.[106] Next, while Gilles Deleuze claims to find in mythos the founding rationale of the paranoia of the *régime* Ricoeur contends that myth constitutes the communal work of constructing an intelligible world.[107] Jean-François Lyotard powerfully argues that narrative finality constitutes a coercive imposition of a last word on a potentially limitless heterogeneity.[108] Yet Ricoeur continues with a positive—dare we say Hegelian—view of the teleological structure of narrative. Finally, Philippe Lacoue-Labarthe argues that mimesis embodies *la force identificatoire* of myth whose epistemological and historical point of no return is the Nazi narrative of the *Volk;*

---

[104] Returning to a point made in note 8 above, the question which remains unresolved, and seemingly unresolvable, is whether or not Ricoeur's transcendental idealism in presupposing that certain necessary *a priori* conditions constitute the very possibility of human willing assumes not only certain "epistemic" conditions, but two distinctive conditions of being. The query remains: Does his dual-aspect account assume two realms of being *or* simply two ways of viewing the same being? It seems that evidence could be found in Ricoeur to support both answers—and in theory both could be true, but the less problematical alternative is accepting only an epistemological distinction. We could, then, say that consistent with the hermeneutical aim of mediating self-knowledge, a dual-aspect account of the human subject offers us the conditions for representing our experiences by way of signs, symbols, and myths. See page 73 above on possible ontological conditions.

[105] Ricoeur, "The Narrative Function," in *Hermeneutics and the Human Sciences,* pp. 274–96; and Jean-Paul Sartre, *The Words,* trans. Bernard Frechtman (New York: Vintage Books, 1981).

[106] Roland Barthes, *Mythologies,* trans. Annette Lavers (London: Jonathan Cape, 1972).

[107] Gilles Deleuze and Felix Guattari, *A Thousand Plateaus,* trans. Brain Massumi (London: Athlone, 1987).

[108] Jean-François Lyotard, *The differend: phrases in dispute,* trans. George Van Den Abbeele (Minneapolis: University of Minnesota Press, 1988), pp. 151–52, 155–56.

but Ricoeur contends that the mimetic activity of myth reflects the structure of care.[109]

For Ricoeur, in sharp criticism with radical—and, for many, decisive—criticisms of mythical narratives, *mythos* is definitely not a negative term. In fact Ricoeur maintains that narrative emplotment whether it be mythical or historical is a form of human knowledge. This means that, for him, knowledge is inextricably linked to time. More precisely, knowledge is the product of human work upon time; it is the active shaping of the otherwise formless character of pure succession into narrative form.

Alongside of other, postmodern readings of Kant's Enlightenment legacy, Ricoeur's claim, in *Time and Narrative*, is epistemologically daring. Essentially Ricoeur claims that the historical and mythical configurations with which we shape our lives continue to have real cognitive power. Comprehending our experience as human beings in time depends upon the configuring act of narrative representation. "Time becomes human to the extent that it is articulated through a narrative mode, and narrative attains its full meaning when it becomes a condition of temporal existence."[110]

Ricoeur distinguishes himself from much of his intellectual milieu by rejecting the ahistorical grammar of narrative typologies, especially the typologies favored by early structuralism. He argues that narratives are not only orderings of time, they are also ordered by time; about time, they are also in time. History determines the conditions for dynamic redescription of experience and so for the activity of productive imagination. In the end, though, Ricoeur remains unclear concerning the determining conditions of history and their relation to truth. With the question of truth Ricoeur may come closer to postmodern critiques than even he would admit. As we have seen Ricoeur resists a final synthesis of the tensions inherent in human willing. Moreover his thought is characterized, to a certain degree, by the deferral of meaning and the non-closure of history. Our desciption of the peculiar temporal condition of human willing has led to the conclusion that human beings can never achieve the highest good which, nevertheless, remains the object of their will. The ideal of a kingdom of God must, therefore, always remain eschatological.

---

[109] Philippe Lacoue-Labarthe, *Heidegger, Art and Politics*, trans. Chris Turner (Oxford: Basil Blackwell, 1990); and Ricoeur, "Narrative Time," *Critical Inquiry*, vol. 7, no. 1 (autumn 1980), p. 181.

[110] Ricoeur, *Time and Narrative*, I, p. 52.

3

Ricoeur's Symbolic Account of Human and Divine

The stage has been reached for elaborating my third claim: that a dialectical relationship between human and divine is both constituted by and constitutive of the ontological and eschatological conditions of Ricoeur's christology. Elaboration of this third claim queries the possibility of conceiving a relationship between human sin as represented by the first Adam and divine grace as revealed in the second Adam. The myths of the first and second Adam, in portraying a human bond with the sacred, serve us as paradigms for Ricoeur's post-Kantian christology. Yet the critical question is, What concept of grace, if any, can be formulated and legitimized on the basis of Ricoeur's philosophy of the will which stresses the autonomy of human willing?

According to the dual-aspect account of experience presented in the previous chapter, human willing involves freedom and rationality. Human beings are not merely characterized by fissiparously diverse inclinations and desires. In fact it can be said that we are also, on philosophical principle and in existential fact, able to recognize ourselves, in Kantian terms, as autonomous in the noumenal choice of the fundamental disposition which is the unifying maxim of all moral action. If there is this free choice, then in what sense is divine grace as the gift of complete freedom necessary?

Ricoeur admits that, as quoted in the previous chapter, it is not possible to comprehend how the archetype of the good principle has established itself in humankind. In Kantian terms he points to the incomprehensible yet necessary ground for conceiving abstractly of "the good principle which struggles within us with the evil principle," and for speaking concretely of Christ who "suffers for the universal good."[1] Thus Ricoeur speaks both symbolically of the gift of freedom and critically of the myths concerning the first and second Adam. Yet does Ricoeur's critical restoration of the biblical symbols and myths come any closer to resolving the related question of truth?

In his 1969 review of *The Symbolism of Evil*, John Hick raises this question:

> [Ricoeur's]program is a philosophical hermeneutics of myth and symbol. Its presupposition is that the truth is already contained, although hidden, in the primitive human reactions to the world which are embodied in man's myths. This is an enormous assumption. What grounds are there for thinking it to be true?

Hick also insists that

> Ricoeur deliberately restricts himself to the description and analysis of the myths that have been prevalent within different cultures and does not raise, except marginally, the ultimately crucial question of what the response of Christian thought should be to the mystery of evil.[2]

Hick is correct insofar as Ricoeur does analyse four mythical types concerning the origin and end of evil; and Ricoeur does not seem to seek a correct, normative response to the mystery of evil within the tradition. Yet it has been maintained by Kevin Vanhoozer, for instance, that Ricoeur engages in theological controversies in order to achieve a mediating position which would speak to what the response of Christian thought should be;[3] presumably, then, Ricoeur's answer to Hick would be to find a position somewhere between opposing myths on evil. However I would make an important distinction, notwithstanding Vanhoozer and Hick.

If Ricoeur's ability to achieve mediating positions is to be considered philosophically interesting and theologically significant, then it would be in his ability to express unexpressed relations between apparently different positions rather than to achieve, or seek to achieve, an absolute

---

[1] Ricoeur, "Freedom in the Light of Hope," *The Conflict of Interpretations*, p. 424.

[2] John Hick, "Review of *Symbolism of Evil*," *Theology Today*, vol. 24, no. 4 (1969), pp. 521–522; for a more complete discussion of the early and the recent Hick see my "Ricoeur and Hick on Evil: Post-Kantian Myth?" *Contemporary Philosophy* (1992), p. 17

[3] Kevin Vanhoozer, *Biblical Narrative in the Philosophy of Paul Ricoeur* (Cambridge: Cambridge University Press, 1990). pp. 4–7, 11–13, 226–27, 257–65, 275, 279–87.

reconciliation between warring camps.[4] I submit that a great injustice is done to Ricoeur when one assesses his theological reflections, as Vanhoozer does and as the early Hick seems to want to do, according to restrictive norms of Christian truth, that is, according to norms which are by definition dogmatic and absolute. It is more appropriate to seek to formulate Ricoeur's response to such a fundamental question as Hick's regarding the mystery of evil in open-ended, post-Kantian terms, i.e. terms which intend to avoid either dogmatism or skepticism. In *The Symbolism of Evil* and *The Conflict of Interpretations* Ricoeur does turn to Kant's description of the inscrutable (*unerforschbar*) nature of the radical evil. This evil corrupts the very ground of all human free willing. So, too, in *Time and Narrative*, III, Ricoeur continues to speak of refiguring the inscrutable.[5]

The last section of this chapter on "Symbolic Reconstruction" returns to the problem of truth. Before this I endeavor to elucidate further Ricoeur's post-Kantian ontology and eschatology. In the sections to follow I, first, present critically his symbolism concerning humankind's captive free will by contrasting it with Augustine's concept of original sin. Second, Ricoeur's unfulfilled ontology[6] of human freedom is presented in terms of a relationship between temporal experience and a non-temporal concept or ideal. To explain the schematization of the good principle in the archetype I show the way in which the second Adam serves as a schematization of the non-temporal concept of freedom; Christ as both human and divine represents the divine as innocent freedom. Third, the primary symbols of evil are reread in relation to the original innocence of the second Adam. In particular the sacrifice of Christ as constituting the symbolic gift of life offers the possibility of bridging the gulf between immanent defilement and transcendent innocence.

Ricoeur's initial statement concerning the antinomy of free will and grace is to be found in the Introduction to *Freedom and Nature*:

> We hope to show the fruitfulness of an "a-logic of paradox" for recasting the old debates about freedom and grace (or predestination). I receive all, and this gift consists in this: that I am complete freedom in the receiving of that

---

[4] I take issue with Vanhoozer who oversimplifies Ricoeur as he who "marches to a conciliatory drummer," or seeks to make peace between warring camps; ibid., pp. 4–5, 286–87.

[5] Ricoeur, *Time and Narrative*, III, pp. 261, 270.

[6] Ricoeur, "Existence and Hermeneutics," pp. 22–24.

gift. But the paradox of freedom and Transcendence can be sustained only
as a mystery which it is the task of a poetics to discern.[7]

The immediate challenge is to recast the notion of complete freedom as
gift, and at the same time to sustain the paradox of freedom and
transcendence as mystery.[8] Ricoeur's reference to the old debates about
freedom and grace (or predestination) is contextualized in his
hermeneutical study of Augustine. This will be the focus of the section
which follows.[9]

I. A Captive Free Will

Ricoeur states his intention to reconstruct the meaning of the debate
concerning free will and grace in *Freedom and Nature* in the terms of an a-
logic of paradox. Later, in *The Symbolism of Evil*, he contends that a
recourse to symbolism is necessary, in order to grasp the central paradox
of a captive free will (*un libre arbitre captif*):

> the symbolic and non-literal character of the captivity of sin and the
> infection of defilement becomes quite clear when these symbols are used to
> denote a dimension of freedom itself... Why this recourse to...symbolism?
> Because the paradox of a captive free will—the paradox of a *servile will*—is
> insupportable for thought.[10]

His statement on the paradox of freedom and grace in the same work
recalls St Paul's symbolism of the irreducible contrasts written into the
arguments of *Romans* 5:20, 11:32:

> it [the text of *Romans*] emphasizes the divine origin of...liberty... After
> the event, the delivered conscience recognizes in the ethical stage,
> experienced as slavery, the tortuous road to its liberation; but...the
> paradox... [of freely sinning and yet of obtaining grace] can be read only
> from the top downward.[11]

The phrase used by Ricoeur from the top downward refers back to
his interpretation of Paul's argument as moving from the

---

[7] Ricoeur, *Freedom and Nature*, p. 33.

[8] Ricoeur, *Gabriel Marcel et Karl Jaspers*, pp. 63, 259.

[9] Ricoeur, "'Original Sin': A Study in Meaning," trans. Peter McCormick, in *The Conflict of Interpretations*, pp. 269–86.

[10] Ricoeur, *The Symbolism of Evil*, p. 152.

[11] Ibid., p. 149.

superabundance of grace in the second Adam to recognition of the abundance of sin in the first Adam. A fundamental and crucial point for Ricoeur's restoration of the myths concerning the first and second Adam (which includes the symbolism of sin, captivity, and redemption) is that sin—and similarly the first Adam—can only be understood retrospectively and symbolically in the light of the innocence and grace of God as represented by the second Adam.[12]

However it is a particular statement in "La Rochelle Confessions of Faith of the Reformed Churches" that the will of man is totally captive to sin which leads Ricoeur back to a reconsideration of its early formulation in Augustine.[13] What is especially significant for Ricoeur about Augustine's polemical writings in the early fifth century is his development of a particular understanding of original sin:

> Saint Augustine witnesses to the great historical moment when this concept is formed. Augustine first led the battle against the Manichaeans and then against the Pelagians. And in this battle on two fronts the polemical and apologetic concept of original sin was developed. But my work is not the work of a historian. It is not the history of the anti-Manichaean polemic and then the anti-Pelagian polemic which interests me... I am, then, neither a dogmatic theologian nor a historian; I would like, very precisely, to contribute to what I will call a hermeneutics of the so-called dogma of original sin. This interpretation, which is reductive on the epistemological level but recuperative on the symbolic level, is a development of what I have elsewhere attempted under the title *The Symbolism of Evil*. It moves the criticism of theological language from the level of *images and mythical symbols* like "captivity," "fall," "error," "perdition," "rebellion," etc. to that of *rational symbols*.[14]

A major difficulty for contemporary theologians with Augustine's discussions concerning sin is that the beginning of evil is literally dated from Adam's first sin. As Ricoeur argues, Adam represents a figure in a myth that must not be identified with one particular historical person, but with humankind in general. Ricoeur's interpretation of the Adamic myth does not serve as the model for the Christ myth. Conversely, in *The Symbolism of Evil* he claims that the historicity or the historical understanding of Christ as the second Adam informs interpretation of

---

[12] Ibid., pp. 173, 235–43.

[13] Ricoeur, "Existence and Hermeneutics," p. 26; *Confession de foi de la Rochelle* (1959), article 9.

[14] Ibid., pp. 271–72; cf. *The Symbolism of Evil*, pp. 4–10, 237.

the first Adam.[15] So sin is grasped retrospectively and symbolically which means that the first Adam's story is only fully understood in the light of the historical narrative concerning the second Adam.

The term myth does not have the same function when Ricoeur uses it in relation to Christ as when used to refer to the *Genesis* account of the fall of Adam. Ricoeur assumes that an eschatological myth of salvation, especially as represented in Pauline theology, serves as the type to the primordial myth of Adam's fall, which then becomes the anti-type.[16] Also the Christ myth, different from the Adamic myth, constitutes part of a unique historical narrative. What is seen as common to the symbolic representations of both Christ and Adam, and what is said to characterize each as myth, are the ways in which the universal and the individual or, from a transcendental idealist point of view, the non-temporal conditions and temporal experiences are brought together in the imaginative reconstruction of a lived story.

The construction of the second Adam narrative develops from the temporal particularities of the individual life of Christ to a universal mythical sense. The narrative representation of the first Adam, in contrast, moves from a universal mythical sense to the individual aspects of a spatio-temporal story which could be yours or mine. Both the first and second Adams as symbolic representations of human experience, then, unite spatio-temporal intuitions with a non-temporal concept by way of the telling of a mythical story. I take this common power to connect the universal sense of the non-temporal and the individual aspects of human temporality as the ground for identifying the Adamic and Christological narratives alike as being myths.

In addition to Ricoeur's different uses of myth, a possibly contentious point is made concerning myth and history. Due to its typological relationship to the second Adam narrative the Yahwist account of the creation of the first Adam in *Genesis* is conceivable, according to Ricoeur, as a broken and historicized myth. Such a conception of myth is developed by Ricoeur in "Myth and History."[17]

> The "historical" understanding of a people through its literature is not exclusively, nor even principally, expressed in historiographic writings ...expansion of the historical mind beyond the narrative form characteristic

---

[15] Ricoeur, *The Symbolism of Evil*, pp. 173, 235–43, 275.

[16] Ricoeur, "Structure and Hermeneutics," trans. Kathleen McLaughlin, in *The Conflict of Interpretations*, pp. 27–61 especially "The Limits of Structuralism," 44–45; cf. *The Symbolism of Evil*, pp. 172–73, 272–78.

[17] Ricoeur, "Myth and History," pp. 273–82.

of historiography finds its expression in the internal hierarchy characteristic of the narrative literature of the Hebrew scriptures, through which the narrative units distinguished by the typology are subordinated to large ensembles, of which the Yahwist document is a good model... [but] we must admit that...the notion of myth...[in] its strict sense of a history of origins *in illo tempore*... unfolds...in the time of the gods... Would we then be justified in speaking of a return to mythical time by way of a history-like narrative, on the basis of the theologies presiding over the narrative composition itself, as, for example, in the conception of history as salvation history? This could be done only by ascribing to the term myth the extremely broad sense of a founding narrative that is related to everyday existence. In fact, it is just as important to stress the historicization of myth as it is to emphasize the mythologization of history. The position of the origin myth in *Genesis* 1–11 attests to this decisive subordination of myth to history...as a broken and historicized myth.[18]

A discussion of the debatable conception of history as "salvation history" (*Heilesgeschichte*) will not be given.[19] But it can be admitted that if the Adamic myth, understood as a broken and historicized myth, represents the historicization of myth, then the Christ myth, conceived as the mythologization of history, represents a parallel movement in the opposite direction. The important point to bear in mind generally in contemporary discussions concerning myth and history is that there exists a discontinuity between historical time and mythical time. This discontinuity is recognized in the fact that mythical time is said to represent the time of the gods, i.e. *in illo tempore*. Unlike historical time which represents the time of humankind and evil, mythical time is characterized by the functioning of the mythico-poetic imagination in portraying as an intelligible whole an original state of innocence, the fall into sin, and a final restoration of innocence.

The decisive problem for Ricoeur with Augustine's use of original sin as a concept is the result of two main factors. First, Ricoeur is ultimately not able to accept Augustine's Neo-Platonic account of human desire and reason. Second, he obviously rejects Augustine's interpretation of the Adamic story as actual history.

---

[18] Ibid., pp. 279–81.

[19] The German word *Heilsgeschichte*—salvation or redemptive history—is first employed as a technical term in theology during the nineteenth-century. In fact Ricoeur refers to the revival of this now debatable conception of history in the twentieth-century by Oscar Cullmann, *Christ and Time*, trans. Floyd Filson (London: SCM, 1951) and by Gerhard von Rad in *Old Testament Theology* trans. D. M. G. Stalker (Edinburgh: Oliver and Boyd, 1962); *The Symbolism of Evil*, pp. 262–77.

It is necessary to explain, however briefly, in what way Augustine's theology of original sin and his hierarchy of human desires are incompatible with Ricoeur's post-Kantian reconstruction of human reason and desire. In Kantian terms desire is always associated with the sensible world;[20] the highest good as the entire object of the will is conceived to be the harmonious connection of desire and reason. The highest good is, according to Ricoeur, ideally represented by the second Adam. But, for Augustine, desire, in its highest employment, goes beyond all transient desire of the sensible world. Through contemplation of the eternal God, human beings should be able to separate themselves from physical or natural inclinations which can never be rightly ordered as ends in themselves. It is not that the created world is without value for Augustine, but he considers love of any creature as inordinate if it is not tempered by the absolute love of God that gives the proper balance to human desires. Love of God has to be accorded the highest place in a hierarchy of desires; only if this is so can human desires for love and physical satisfaction be given their due (relative) proportions.

Also consider the implications of Ricoeur's rejection of Augustine's interpretation of original sin based, as it is, upon a connection with a particular historical event. Following Augustine the use of original sin as a theological concept cannot, in the light of Ricoeur's hermeneutics of symbols and myths, be intellectually legitimized. Ricoeur argues that Augustine's idea of original sin is incorrectly employed as a concept if it is literally understood to be the original evil condition of human generation. Yet Ricoeur maintains that it can still have a positive role to play as a symbol. Although rejecting a literal-historical interpretation of *Genesis* which would take sin to be a condition directly caused by Adam, Ricoeur seeks to legitimize a symbolic interpretation of the *Genesis* narratives concerning the ontological condition of sin.

Ricoeur contributes to both criticizing and restoring the meaning of Augustine's account of sin. In accord with various theologians, Ricoeur endeavors to criticize the Augustinian interpretation of original sin while, at the same time, he intends to reconstruct an account of sin which would be consistent with a post-Kantian interpretation of human desire and of biblical myths. In particular, Ricoeur's phenomenological-

---

[20] Granted desire in Kant may be pathological or moral (i.e. when aligned with reason), but whatever the case it is always sensuous, since at the very least "felt" as an aspect of the bodily. For further references to desire in Kant, see Robert Sullivan, *Immanuel Kant's Moral Theory* (Cambridge: Cambridge University Press, 1989), pp. 26–28, 32–33, 118–21, 132–33, 334; also Allison, *Kant's Theory of Freedom*, p. 35, 108–9.

symbolic reading of the experience of evil and sin in *The Symbolism of Evil* reveals that Christians, after Augustine, often came to believe—wrongly—that sin begins with the defilement that occurs as a result of the tainted contact of sexuality. He criticizes a popular misunderstanding of original sin which, in this light, only reflects the basic dilemma implicit in Augustinian theory.

The account of original sin of which Ricoeur is critical—yet by which, nevertheless, he is still influenced—can be briefly characterized as follows. Evil, if inherited through birth, has to be innate in men and women. Yet every human being is still thought to be responsible for evil doing. Although each particular act is completely free, evil action is still unavoidable. It appears, then, that every evil action re-enacts the fall. Ultimately humankind has lost the ability to attain purpose in life or to overcome evil doing and sin without confession to God of native human inadequacy. Original sin has meant for many Christians, and most probably those believers who accept the "La Rochelle Confessions of Faith of the Reformed Church," that due to the fall all humankind has an innate desire to do evil and naturally cannot do anything sufficient on its own to restore the moral or spiritual condition of human beings.[21]

Not surprisingly Ricoeur's characteristic negotiation of conflicting interpretations means that his critical relationship to Augustine is not one which amounts to a total opposition. Instead Ricoeur's symbolism of a captive free will is in part informed by Augustine's profound expression of the dialectical relationship between the temporal and the non-temporal as developed in *The Confessions*. This autobiographical work of Augustine is especially significant for reconstructing, in narrative form, the experience of sin. The narrative reflects an unshakeable and unconditioned belief in a non-temporal reality distinct from human temporality.

For instance, Book XI of *The Confessions* begins with a query concerning the temporal record of his sins. This record is presented to God who is deemed to exist outside of time: "O Lord, since you are outside time in eternity, are you unaware of the things that I tell you? Or do you see in time the things that occur in it? If you see them, why do I lay this lengthy record before you? Certainly it is not through me that you first hear of these things."[22] After several extended reflections about

---

[21] Ricoeur, "'Original Sin,'" p. 269; cf. *Confessions de foi de la Rochelle*, articles 9–11.

[22] Augustine, *The Confessions*, trans. with an introduction by R.S. Pine-Coffin (Harmondsworth: Penguin, 1961), p. 253.

the nature of time, its creation and meaning for human experience, Augustine confesses to his God:

> You, my Father, are eternal. But I am divided between time gone by and time to come, and its course is a mystery to me. My thoughts, the intimate life of my soul, are torn this way and that in the havoc of change. And so it will be until I am purified and melted by the fire of your love and fused into one with you. ...
>
> O Lord my God, how deep are your mysteries! How far from your safe haven have I been cast away by the consequences of my sins! ...Your knowledge ...is not like the knowledge of a man who sings words well known to him or listens to another singing a familiar psalm. While he does this, his feelings vary and his senses are divided, because he is partly anticipating words still to come and partly remembering words already sung. It is far otherwise with you, for you are eternally without change, the truly eternal Creator of minds. ...in the Beginning you created heaven and earth, and there was no change in your action. Some understand this and some do not.[23]

Augustine's confession as a sinner to the effect that "I am divided between time gone by and time to come, and its course is a mystery to me" undoubtedly reflects the consciousness of a temporal being, of a created being. In contrast to the eternal creator the penitent recognizes himself or herself dispersed and torn asunder by the many, discordant moments of temporal experience. Similarly certain biblical narratives can be interpreted as portraying what Ricoeur identifies in Augustine as the phenomenological distention of experience, i.e. experience stretched between past and future without a unifying intention. The portrayal of distention in the Bible appears particularly in relation to the past with images of the wandering of the Old Adam. Old Testament images of dissolution, blindness, and deviation are opposed to the symbolism of eternity with its figures of immortality, light, and steadfastness.

For Ricoeur, the potential relationship of a temporal being to eternity is reflected in the unifying intention of Augustine in reciting a psalm. However it is important to note that, in sharp contrast to this, what might be called a postmodern or deconstructive reading of Augustine's recitation of the very same psalm would seek to undermine the relationship of the text to the supposed non-temporal authority. That is, a deconstructive reading would dismantle the Author-authored relationship; for example, Ralph Flores' deconstruction of Augustine's

---

[23] Ibid., pp. 279–80.

rhetoric exposes the doubtful character of the authority to which the text has been related.[24]

Despite any such postmodern readings Ricoeur's phenomeno-logical interpretation of the psalm-recitation insists upon the role of present consciousness in unifying the memory of the past and expectation of the future. Although the alienation of a sinner in time appears even as the psalm is being recited, that is, as the distention of the very same human memory and expectation, an unifying intention of the recitation still constitutes the ground of hope for the last things. Salvation is revealed to the extent that the sinful past is remembered as the figure of the old Adam[25] and the future is anticipated as the figure of the new man in Christ.[26]

Certainly, for Augustine, an account of the connection between time and eternity—as well as that between sin and salvation—is inevitably a mysterious one based, as it is, upon a Neo-Platonic dualism.[27] Yet Ricoeur reconstructs Augustine so that he anticipates a phenomenological analysis of internal-time consciousness whereby the present is necessarily made up of both past and future.[28] This idea of a threefold present suggests that human consciousness is seen in Husserlian terms as essentially constituting time in a subjective (or intuitive) apprehension of its intentional structure.

Not only does Ricoeur bring into question an accepted interpretation of Augustine's concept of original sin, but he attempts to go beyond what he identifies as the enigmatic nature of Augustine's account of time. Ironically Ricoeur remains caught up in the idealist problematic concerning temporality and non-temporality.

Just as Ricoeur is partly indebted to Augustine for his development of the contrast between temporal sinning and non-temporal sinlessness, so also his understanding of sin as offence against a holy will has antecedents in Augustine. As intimated above Ricoeur finds a rich source of interrogative thought represented in such historical narratives and symbols as are to be found in *The Confessions*. These are narrative

---

[24] Ricoeur, *Time and Narrative*, I; and Ralph Flores, *The Rhetoric of Doubtful Authority* (Ithaca: Cornell University Press, 1984), pp. 44–65.

[25] George Steiner suggests that Ricoeur's ontological fictions help to understand the repressed past and to move beyond the guilt produced by this past; see *After Babel* (Oxford: Oxford University Press, 1975), p. 134n.

[26] Cf. *Romans* 5 & *Philippians* 3: 13.

[27] A.H. Armstrong, "St Augustine and Christian Platonism," in R.A. Markus (ed.), *Augustine: A Collection of Critical Essays* (Garden City, NY: Doubleday, 1972), pp. 3–37.

[28] Ricoeur, *Time and Narrative*, I, pp. 5–30.

accounts constituted by the experience of which a penitent makes confession.[29] In addition Ricoeur again sees a similarly significant narration of an experience of sin is found in the oldest Babylonian psalter in which a penitent addresses himself to a mysterious, hidden god asking: "How long, O Lord? What god have I sinned against? What sin have I committed."[30] Ricoeur stresses that the blind and complex character of the experiences recounted in ancient as well as in more recent confessions of sin needs to be understood in the light of known or unknown offence(s) against a holy will.

As previously stated, Ricoeur sees in human avowal a fundamental awareness of the fault, i.e. the disproportion of humankind within its self. As a further level of this awareness of faulted existence sin makes me incomprehensible to myself.[31] It is essential that my sin, in this context, be understood in the absolute sight of the eternal, holy will of an omniscient God. This recalls the crucial point that sin can only be understood retrospectively in the light of the limiting ideas of God as a gift of transcendence or as a highest good.

> the primordial significance of this seeing is to constitute the *truth* of my situation, the justness and the justice of the ethical judgment that can be passed on my existence. That is why this seeing, far from preventing the birth of the Self, gives rise to self-awareness; ...this seeing which is, lays the foundation for the ought-to-be of self-awareness.[32]

Despite certain debts to Augustine, Ricoeur's description of the awareness of the self's sinful condition owes, I insist, its greatest debt to and presupposes Kant's account of moral experience. In this case, he recalls the ethical distinction between what I ought to do and what I in fact do. This distance is only made comprehensible, according to Ricoeur, by Kant who develops the conceptual framework which Augustine lacks. (At the same time it needs to be conceded that Augustine's rich narrative insight concerning the distention and intention of the human soul, such as that quoted above from *The Confessions*, has no parallel in Kant's philosophy.)

Admittedly Augustine, in *Contra Felicem Manichaeum*, attempted to explain evil strictly with reference to the human will. However, in order

---

[29] Ricoeur, *The Symbolism of Evil*, p. 8.
[30] Ibid.
[31] Ricoeur, *Fallible Man*, pp. xxv–xxviii, 4, 144, 200; also *The Symbolism of Evil*, pp. 3, 170–71, 312.
[32] Ricoeur, *The Symbolism of Evil*, p. 85.

not to confuse evil with material nature he argued that it is not a something and that one should not ask "what is evil?" (*quid est malum?*), but "whence do we do evil?" (*unde malum faciamus?*). Ricoeur contends that Augustine lacked the conceptual framework to avoid confusing the evil will with an evil nature.[33] In particular, Augustine's argument against the Pelagians concerning original sin tends to make biological nature, that is, concupiscence at conception, the vehicle of inherited evil; and so the taint of sin is presumed to be inherited through birth.

As demonstrated in the last chapter, but now seen in a contrast with Augustine, Kant specified various dynamic aspects of the human will. These involve the practical concepts of *Wille* and *Willkür*, as well as the *Maxim* or principle of the will. The *Maxim* that serves as the subjective ground of all its moral action must be freely chosen by *Willkür*. Different from *Willkür*, *Wille* does not act temporally or adopt maxims but introduces the moral law into the experience of willing. These practical concepts are used in Kant's discussion of radical evil to demonstrate the manner in which the dynamic workings of the distinct aspects of the human will give rise to the propensity to evil as the perversion of the ultimate subjective ground of the adoption of all moral maxims. With this conceptual framework Kant is able to succeed where Augustine failed insofar as he avoided any equation of evil with either human sensible nature or human reason alone.

Ricoeur, following this reading of Kant, is able to maintain that evil does not reside in sensibility; neither does it arise from a complete perversion of the rational. Rather evil comes about when the free will (*Willkür*) adopts a maxim which subordinates the pure rational motive, respect for the moral law, to sensible motives. The ground of this opposition of the free will to moral law cannot be known. The propensity—or subjective ground of the possibility of an inclination—to evil in human nature may reveal itself in the tension between the temporality of nature and the non-temporality implicit in the initiation of free action; but no inductive proof could ever elucidate the essence of this propensity. Ricoeur refers to a statement from Kant's *Religion* which would imply a non-temporal, unknowable ground of evil: "Even if the *Dasein* of this propensity can be demonstrated (*dargetan*) by empirical proofs of conflict in time, the nature (*Beschaffenheit*) and ground (*Grund*)

---

[33] Ricoeur, "'Original Sin,'" pp. 273–76.

of this propensity must be apprehended *a priori*, for it is a relation of freedom to law, the concept of which is always non-empirical."[34]

Again Kant's account of the inscrutable origin of evil in the *Religion* supports Ricoeur's reliance on symbolic language in representing the evil will. This also enables Ricoeur to recognize in the biblical myths a theory of evil radically different from Augustine's. The assertion may be made that Kant's account in the essay "On the Radical Evil in Human Nature" accords with the biblical narrative in proposing that evil, although inscrutable, can be represented as a temporal condition of humankind. The myth of a fall is understood to depict humankind's relationship, or loss of relationship, to a non-temporal reality. According to Kant the Adamic myth needs to be interpreted symbolically as portraying a fall through its account of a quasi-event arising from an unknowable non-temporal source and as representing the temptation of every man and woman.

In stark contrast with Augustine who thought that the origin of evil could be explained, Kant emphasized that the crucial mythical figure of the serpent represents the unfathomable origin of evil. The serpent's role in the seduction of Eve illustrates that evil is not strictly speaking innate, but that it arises from outside human consciousness. Equally, the mythical event signifies the contingent, historical (i.e. temporal) nature of radical evil. Although the penitent recognizes and so confesses the radical nature of his or her evil actions, the myth does not depict the human subject of evil-doing as possessing a primordially evil nature but, instead, portrays the origin of the propensity to radical evil as being ineluctably inscrutable. Satan, then, represents the inscrutable. At the same time, the contingency of evil leaves open the possibility that sinfulness is connected with temporality and that, despite being sinful, humankind still derives its being from a non-temporal reality.

Ricoeur's post-Kantian account of human willing provides the conceptual framework to criticize Augustine's use of original sin as a concept and, at the same time, to restore its employment as a symbol. For Ricoeur, the truth for every man and woman of the myths of the first and second Adam is to recognize sin as a symbol which represents a universal—yet also a temporal—condition of humankind. Ricoeur's central counter-assertion to the Augustinian claim that original sin is the result of the actual fall of a historical individual (i.e. Adam) is offered in

---

[34] Ricoeur, "The Hermeneutics of Symbol and Philosophical Reflection, I" trans. Denis Savage, in *The Conflict of Interpreations*, p. 307; cf. *Religion within the Limits of Reason Alone*, pp. 30–31.

The Symbolism of Evil. It is in the light of the mythical symbolism concerning the origin and the end of evil that the following counter-assertion by Ricoeur must be understood: "However *radical* evil may be, it cannot be as *primordial* as goodness."[35] In other words, no matter how original sin or the fault may be from the point of view of everyday experience or, from a literal-historical interpretation of *Genesis*, according to Ricoeur freedom is always more original.

Keeping in mind the above counter-assertion it may be asked if Ricoeur is right to speak, along with Kant, of a radical evil in human nature? In order to answer this question allow me to elucidate another important although problematical idea which Ricoeur appropriates from the *Religion.* That is, human beings as dual-aspect beings are ultimately destined for goodness as represented in Christ, the archetype of the pure moral disposition, but are also inclined like the mythical first Adam to evil. The question, then, is: If all human beings possess the propensity to radical evil and so corrupt the very ground of their maxims how can anyone possessed of this evil disposition ever actually be worthy of happiness or agree with the maxim of holiness? Kant's answer seems to be that there always remains hope, despite a corrupt heart, that humankind, while still possessing a free will, might return to a good disposition. How, then, in the light of this tension between propensity for radical evil and "destination" (*Bestimmung*) for goodness might Ricoeur's perspective on freedom and grace be reconstructed? Any serious attempt to answer this question has to reconstruct Ricoeur's mythical representation of an innocent freedom.

II. The Non-temporal Concept of Freedom

A contention of the previous chapter is that Ricoeur's dual-aspect account of human willing supports both the compatibility of freedom and determinism and their incompatibility. To make this theologically and existentially intelligible Ricoeur speaks symbolically of freedom and evil. As Michael Arbib and Mary Hesse explain,

> [Ricoeur's] Biblical [symbols] for evil are drawn from the prisoner and the outcast: bondage, slavery to self and to sin, alienation from God (see the discussion in Ricoeur, *The Symbolism of Evil*, Part I). Freedom is described in opposite [symbolism], as casting aside all weights and oppression,"

---

[35] Ricoeur, *The Symbolism of Evil*, p. 156; as previously noted this assertion appears earlier in a slightly different form in *Fallible Man*, p. 222.

"running the race of the liberty of the children of God" who seeks us as a father or lover. Freedom is...a *telos* to be achieved in the destiny of each human being to become his or her true self in communion with God and with others.[36]

In order to assess more fully and critically the biblical symbolism which Ricoeur takes to express the ideas of freedom and evil, it is necessary to return to his post-Kantian conceptual framework. Now Ricoeur's transcendental idealist categories of the temporal and the non-temporal are undeniably problematical. Do these categories refer to two distinct realms of being? Or do they simply describe being from two different points of view? Whatever answer we might give to such queries, these categories clearly inform Ricoeur's understanding of the dialectical relationship between human and divine. The fundamental problem is that Ricoeur's transcendental idealism renders inevitable a contradictory account of human willing as temporal and non-temporal.

Unwittingly or not, Ricoeur demonstrates that time itself constitutes the fundamental bipolarity of human willing. This is evident in the manner in which the order of temporal succession serves a crucial role in Ricoeur's account of human freedom. "Freedom does not," he insists, "belong exclusively to rational motives sweeping away affective motives (or inclinations)."[37] Nor, he adds, does it "belong exclusively to the surge from the deep which breaks through anonymous dead, intellectual reason." On the contrary, it occurs "whenever I am in command of the succession [of discrete temporal moments], when the shifting focus is in my power."[38] Yet in what sense can it be said that the human subject is "in command of the succession" of spatio-temporally determined moments and when is "the shifting of focus...in my power?"

In addition, we come up against at least two different views on human temporality which render this account even more problematical. First, Ricoeur's multi-leveled description of human willing involves a conception of the human subject as being rationally free, but embodied— and so constrained. This description recalls Kant's conception of the

---

[36] Michael Arbib and Mary Hesse, *The Construction of Reality* (Cambridge: University Cambridge Press, 1986), p. 102. In this quotation I have replaced "metaphor" with "symbol" in order to be consistent with Ricoeur's own usage in *The Symbolism of Evil*, pp. 151–57; for further discussion on symbol and metaphor see Ricoeur, *Interpretation Theory: Discourse and the Surplus of Meaning* (Fort Worth: Texas Christian University Press, 1976), pp. 45–70.

[37] Ricoeur, *Freedom and Nature*, p. 150.

[38] Ibid.

crucial function of the imagination which mediates between temporal intuitions and non-temporal concepts. Second, Ricoeur's analysis of willing presupposes Husserl's subjective analysis of internal-time consciousness.

According to Kant's account of human experience in the first *Critique* pre-temporal intuitions are received and the imagination generates time by bringing successive appearances under a rule of unity.[39] Following this, Ricoeur's analysis of willing takes into account the natural inclinations or desires that motivate a decision to act. For Ricoeur human willing is always governed by the incarnation of the subject within a temporally determined order. Yet, as he also states, the marks of the human subject are found in certain aspects of change itself which cannot be fully explained by the flux of the radically involuntary. We arrive at a point which depends again upon Kant and Husserl.

Unlike Kant's presupposition concerning the unsynthesized discrete pre-temporal intuitions of sensibility, the intuitive time presupposed by Husserl's phenomenology grasps the distention of the present as the retention of the past and the protention of the future. This means that, in Ricoeur's words,

> time is the *flux* of the present. Now each present has by its very nature a horizon of anticipation (or, as Husserl has it, of protention) and a horizon of memory or, better, in the broadest sense of the word, of retention. "The present is unceasingly *becoming* an other present," that means, "each anticipated future *becomes* present" and "the present becomes retained past." These three... are not disparate but all of a piece; memory grows because there is always a present becoming a past and there is always a present because there is always a future which points to the horizon.[40]

However, in assuming Kant's transcendental idealism Ricoeur presupposes that the human subject must be understood as both an object which, like any other empirical object, is known by way of the forms of time and space and as a subject which is involved in constituting time as a plurality of discrete moments on the way to becoming united by the power of the transcendental imagination. In contrast to Ricoeur's assumptions concerning internal-time consciousness, as seen in the above, time also serves as a form of self-alienation and dispersion:

---

[39] Cf. Kant, *Critique of Pure Reason*, A100–1, A142–44.

[40] Ricoeur, *Freedom and Nature*, p. 151.

Change constantly makes me other than myself. This dialectic between
the same I want to be and the other which I become takes place daily in
each of us: anyone who commits himself confronts his own change and
discovers the ruinous process. My own metamorphoses are enigmatic
and discouraging. Now this change is equally dispersion. My life is
naturally discontinuous...life is more often a cacophony than a melody,
without a unique intention which would give it form from end to end as a
theme for improvization.[41]

In the light of these different descriptions of time, from the very same
work, the human subject both exists in time—and so changes with time—
and either intuits time, according to Husserl, or, alternatively according
to Kant, constitutes time. In fact both Kant and Husserl lend support to
Ricoeur's essentially transcendental idealist conception of the human
subject—a conception deemed by Ricoeur himself to be paradoxical.[42]

According to Husserl's description of internal-time consciousness,
time is stretched to such an extent that human consciousness may be
perceived to be timeless. Yet how, then, can phenomenologists such as
Merleau-Ponty and Ricoeur, both of whom follow Husserl's method of
phenomenological description, also claim that meaning is at once vital—
in the sense of being caught up in time—and intentional in relation to
time? No summary answer to this important question will be proposed.
Neither will an attempt be made to reconcile Husserl's conception of, in
Ricoeur's terms, intuitive time with Kant's invisible time. However such
a reconciliation has been attempted by Ricoeur in *Time and Narrative*, III.

Recognition of this paradoxical account supports my claim that
Ricoeur's philosophy of the will is premissed on a transcendental idealist
problematic. In turn it is this philosophical framework which makes
intelligible my claim that the schematization of the non-temporal concept
of freedom is constituted by mythical figures.

In *Freedom and Nature*, Ricoeur forecasts that he would restore
meaning to the concrete myth of innocence considered as a narrative
about the beginning of human time and bodily existence. In his words,
"there will perhaps never be an empirical approach to innocence, we
must also add that inspection of the fundamental possibilities of man in
fact depends on the concrete myth of innocence."[43] Later in the
development of his empirics of the will, it is an inexorably paradoxical
account of human time which forces Ricoeur to reconsider the temporal

---

41   Ibid., p. 453.
42   Ibid., pp. 26–28.
43   Ibid., p. 28; also *Fallible Man*, pp. xvii–xxi.

origin of the fault and, in the end, to represent human disproportion in mythical terms as the captivity which makes me a slave to myself. At the same time freedom is imagined according to a concrete myth of innocence. That is, for Ricoeur, certain ancient myths—with their narratives, human/divine figures and plot—constitute the schematization of the non-temporal concept of freedom. The divine is represented by the mythico-poetic imagination as innocent freedom. The imagination, in Ricoeur's words, "by recounting stories of primitive innocence, enchants and conjures up that diffuse sense of bodily mystery conjoined with our very essence as being free, without which pure description would be swallowed up in paradox."[44]

Once more Ricoeur's post-Hegelian-Kantianism is obvious inasmuch as a totality is supposed to be represented by the myths of Adam. Incorporated with the first and second Adam are certain historical figures from the Old Testament (including Abraham, Jacob and Joseph).[45] Moreover the myths together represent in the central figure of Adam, i.e. humankind, the concrete universality of both human freedom and evil, as well as the tension of all temporal experience. On the one hand, this myth concentrates all the evil of history in an individual personage and a single act. A singular mythical event, then, symbolizes an instantaneous—timeless—fall of humankind. On the other hand, this myth develops the same event in a drama which involves time. A succession of incidents and the actions of several characters extend the evil event in an interval of time. The myth of the first Adam illustrates the tension within human experience and represents a focal point at the beginning of history for humankind's unity-in-multiplicity.[46]

Ricoeur argues that, although the figure of the first Adam can only acquire its full meaning retrospectively in the light of the second Adam, it is still important to place the Adamic myth within Hebrew history in order to see the figures and images that develop a theology of history.[47] The King, the Shepherd, the Son of David, the Son of Man, and the servant of Yahweh are all figures that anticipate the second Adam and enrich the original figure of the first Adam. The implication is that these figures point to the meaning of the self-temporalization of God.

According to *The Symbolism of Evil* the Son of Man in particular reveals the meaning of God's incarnation in biblical history and so the

---

[44] Ibid.
[45] Ricoeur, *The Symbolism of Evil*, pp. 244, 262–63.
[46] Ibid., p. 244.
[47] Ibid., p. 260f.

instantiation in time of divine innocence. Initially the Son of Man appears in the historical narratives as a transcendent, heavenly figure—"a mysterious personage 'coming from heaven.'"[48] In *Daniel* 7:13 the Son of Man represents the saints of the most high; there the heavenly figure is conceived to be both an individual person and a personification of the collective entity who signifies the holy person or people at the end of time. Instead of representing the first man, the Son of Man foreshadows the one who will come with the remnant of Israel and the whole of true humanity. A twofold function as judge of the world and king of the end of time draws this figure towards the most ultimate future when the true meaning of present humanity will be revealed.

The decisive point seems to be that the Son of Man provides a clue to the mystery of God's incarnation in Jesus Christ. For Ricoeur, Jesus in *Mark* 13:26–27 links his own destiny with the figure symbolized in *Daniel* 7:13.[49] Paradoxically Jesus unites the figure of the Son of Man with the servant of Yahweh who suffers earthly limitations and, finally, the ultimate suffering of crucifixion and death on a cross. The heavenly, transcendent character of the Son of Man as the judge of the just and king of the most high may not seem susceptible of being incarnated in the bodily form of a suffering servant. Yet Jesus, as the second Adam, who unites the heavenly and the earthly, reveals that what is in mythical terms highest above the human can also be seen as what is most inward in the human. If God came down from heaven in a divine self-giving and is glorified with all humanity then it follows that he should be symbolized as the most high Son of Man. If, at the same time, God remains supremely good, then it also follows that he should be represented as sharing the inner sufferings of his creatures as the servant of Yahweh. The biblical figure of the *Ebed Yahweh* introduces the idea of a voluntary, substitutive suffering which means that the heavenly figure of the most high Son of Man identifies himself with humankind.[50] For Ricoeur, Christ represents, in his vicarious suffering, the identity of one human being with all humankind as embodied, fallen beings.

Without comment on other relevant contemporary biblical studies— even highly critical discussions[51]—of his assumed line of interpretation,

---

[48]   Ibid., p. 265.

[49]   Ibid., pp. 265–68, 271.

[50]   Cf. Ricoeur, "Interpretative Narrative," p. 237–57.

[51]   Ricoeur's reading of the Son of Man as a mysterious personage "coming from heaven" and his claim that in *Mark* 13:26–27 Jesus identifies himself with the Son of Man of *Daniel* 7:13 may not be accepted by all New Testament scholars. See Morna

Ricoeur refers to a much debated interpretation of the Son of Man as "he who reveals the great mystery of the incarnation and atonement of Jesus Christ." Yet in Ricoeur's words:

> ...the identity of the Son of Man and men is the great "mystery" revealed in the prophecy of the last judgment upon the sheep and the goats; the verdict is based on the attitude of men toward the lowly, who *are* the Son of Man ... (Matt. 25:40). The Judge of men is identical with me insofar as they come face to face in action and insofar as they are crushed by the "greater" ones. This "mystery" is augmented by another one, to which we have already alluded: in the great act of justification, the Son of Man figures at the same time as judge and as witness, *Parakletos* and *Kategoros*, while Satan is the *Antidikos*, the Adversary—an astonishing end for the figure of the Serpent who, from Tempter, becomes, within the juridical framework of the cosmic judgment, the prosecuting attorney, while the Judge becomes the intercessor; and he becomes the intercessor because he is also the substituted victim. This series of equivalences is the result of the identification of the Son of Man, judge and king at the End, with the suffering servant (Mark 10: 45).[52]

Let us bear in mind the important influence of Kant's *Religion* on Ricoeur. It is possible to argue that Kant's account of biblical symbolism, in particular Books I and IV of the *Religion*, support in a more fundamental sense than any contemporary exegetical study of the Bible ever could Ricoeur's symbolic interpretation of human history as presented in the Old and New Testaments. In Ricoeur's Kantian terms moral experience is seen in relation to the fall which results from what is portrayed mythically in *Genesis* as a free act of human willing in the fated drama of humankind's temporal existence. More generally human history, as consistent with biblical history, reflects the self-awareness of humankind's own incarnation as a sensible and rational being; temporal experience progresses with an ever-increasing awareness of human limitation, conflict and suffering.

Ricoeur's symbolism concerning humankind suggests that a Judaeo-Christian account of experience remains compatible with a Kantian anthropology. In fact, the Kantian account, it could be argued, developed

Hooker, *The Son of Man in Mark: A Study of the Background of the term "Son of Man" and its use in St. Mark's Gospel* (London: SPCK, 1967); Geza Vermes, *Jesus and the World of Judaism* (London: SCM Press, 1983), pp. 89–99; and Barnabas Lindars, *Jesus Son of Man: A Fresh Examination of the Son of Man Sayings in the Gospels in Light of Recent Research* (London: SPCK, 1983).
[52] Ricoeur, *The Symbolism of Evil*, pp. 270–71.

out of the Judaeo-Christian. Biblical history presents the figures of humankind which enhance what Kant shows in the *Religion* to be human self-awareness. The individual is incorporated into figures such as those in the Old Testament of a suffering servant and a Son of Man which represent all men (and women)[53] in the temporal progression from the first Adam to the second Adam. Yet Ricoeur's distinctive and decisive difference from Kant rests in the fact that individual biblical figures are only fully understood, according to him, retrospectively in the light of Jesus Christ's actual life, death and resurrection as representing God's historical transformation of the first Adam story.[54]

For Ricoeur the redemption account in *Romans* 5–6 transforms the first Adam story by means of a striking comparison and contrast with the second Adam. The gift of the second Adam brings life and righteousness, while the trespass of the first Adam brings death and condemnation. The figures which create a contrast between eternal life and temporal death appear with the idea of God's act in *Romans* 5:15. This contrast emphasizes how much greater is the grace of God that abounds through the voluntary gift of the incarnate Christ than the sin of humankind that reigns through the trepass of Adam. Moreover, for Ricoeur, the symbolism representing the temporal connection between the second and the first Adam implies that a final fulfilment of human history, yet to be completely brought about in the resurrection of humankind in Christ, cannot be understood as a simple restoration of the original created order.[55] Christ is represented eschatologically as both judge and advocate which means that God's grace in Christ does not reduce present human responsibility and development. The symbolism of God's grace in Christ points to a cosmic and communal judgment at the end of time.

The redeemable relationship between the one man and the many, the heavenly and the earthly, the eternal and the temporal is schematized here by the mythical two Adams. The second Adam as the archetype of humankind reveals an essential bond between these opposites. In other words Christ himself represents an innocent freedom. The bond with divine innocence and freedom may not be immediately obvious, since it remains obscured by human evil acts, suffering and sin. Yet this bond,

---

[53] The unargued and highly debatable assumption concerning the generic use of *l'homme* may be unsubstantiable. Possibly due in part to the time of writing Ricoeur exhibits no critical awareness of his inevitably patriarchal theology, nor awareness of the importance of a feminist anthropology.

[54] Ibid., pp. 269ff.

[55] Ibid., p. 272.

however enigmatic has an eschatological significance. There is a deferral of meaning to the final cosmic judgment, as symbolized in *Romans*, when at the end of history humankind is condemned or redeemed. The figure of the end who, as the second Adam, represents both the ideal of human fulfilment and original innocence will be reread with the primary symbols of evil.

III. The Primary Symbols of Evil

In order to recast the myths concerning the origin and the end of evil Ricoeur contends that it is necessary to restore meaning to the primary symbols of defilement, sin, and guilt in the light of the symbolism of the second Adam. Yet it can only be helpful to begin by describing the three primary symbols which, he claims, constitute a universal language of avowal or self-confession. Ricoeur maintains that these universal symbols are found to be common to the languages of different Western cultures as seen especially in their myths. Myths, as explained in the previous chapter, are second-degree symbols in that the mythical narratives give further elaboration to the primary symbols. The fundamental importance of these symbols and myths is reflected in Ricoeur's claim that

> there is no direct, non-symbolic language of evil undergone, suffered, or committed; whether man admits his responsibility or claims to be the prey of an evil which takes hold of him, he does so first and foremost in a symbolism whose articulations can be traced out thanks to various rituals of "confession" that the history of religion has interpreted for us.[56]

The meaning of the complex experience of which a penitent confesses, manifests itself in the apparent and latent intentionalities of defilement, sin, and guilt.[57] According to Ricoeur, the symbol's latent meaning gives rise to multiple levels of thought concerning the fault; and the enduring residue of symbolic meaning constitutes cultural memory.[58] The spiritual genesis of Western thought, then, is to be discovered in the symbolism which arises out of a modern consciousness of the fault, as has been particularly manifest in the encounter between the myths of the Greek and Hebrew cultures. Ricoeur accepts the structuralist hypothesis

---

[56] Ricoeur, "The Hermeneutics of Symbols and Philosophical Reflection, I" p. 289.
[57] Cf. Ricoeur, *The Symbolism of Evil*, pp. 7–8, 25–150.
[58] Ibid., p. 20f.

that it is impossible to interpret and critically assess, for instance, the Hebrew myth of the fall without recognising the symbols which structure the other cultures of the ancient Middle East. It is for this reason that he makes contrasting references to the ancient Greek and Hebrew religious rites and their typical myths.[59]

In addition, Ricoeur's phenomenological analysis of myths and symbols tends to bring out the intuitive meaning of temporal experience. In contrast to the objective Kantian time in which the objects of experience are known to exist according to the *a priori* rule of cause and effect, the phenomenological description of subjective time aims to demonstrate that the meaning of human experience is constantly renewed retroactively by new discoveries which become sources of new approaches to the past. Ricoeur claims that "by retroaction from the successive 'nows,' our past never stops changing its meaning; the present appropriation of the past modifies that which motivates us from the depths of the past."[60] There is, thus, always something more to be explicated in the mediating symbols which structure this changing cultural memory.

A contention informing this chapter should be recalled. Ricoeur himself asserts that the fall of Adam—and so human evil—can only be properly understood in the light of the myth of the second Adam. It is incumbent upon the symbolic account of human evil presented in this section that it recognize the way in which Ricoeur both reconstructs the changing cultural contexts of the primary symbols of evil and, as well, seeks to restore meaning to an innocent freedom in terms of Christ's sacrifice. In other words the symbolism concerning the human experience of being bound or captive will be only fully understood retrospectively according to the symbolism of deliverance.

To reiterate, the three primary symbols which, according to Ricoeur, reflect the awareness of human evil are defilement, sin, and guilt. These universal symbols are elaborated by Ricoeur in the context of four typical ancient myths but the focus here will largely be the Hebrew myth. In any case this is the myth which Ricoeur claims is the most adequate for properly understanding humankind's responsibility in doing evil.

---

[59] Ricoeur also includes the Babylonian myth of the origin and the end of evil in his study of the dynamics of myths in Ibid., pp. 306–46. In a later essay he enlarges the scope of the typical myths to include Eastern myths; "Evil" in Mircea Eliade (ed.), *Encyclopedia of Religion*, vol. 5, pp. 199–208.

[60] Ricoeur, *The Symbolism of Evil*, pp. 21–22.

Defilement, as the first of the three primary symbols, is constituted as a symbol by a double intentionality of a first level intention that gives rise to further thought and a second level of possible meaning. Its first intention points to a pre-ethical awareness of a blemish or stain; this consciousness of impurity gives rise to the further meaning of "a quasi-material something that infects as a sort of filth; that harms by invisible properties and that nevertheless works in the manner of a force in the field of our undivided psychic and corporeal existence."[61] Ricoeur's restoration of defilement reconsiders the critical attitude of modern science which attaches little or no significance to a substance-force of evil that does not distinguish between the sacred and the profane. Yet Ricoeur counters the modern scientist by asserting that this meaning of defilement provides a "first sketch of causality": "If you suffer, if you are ill, if you fail, if you die, it is because you have sinned."[62] A Greek fragment of Anaximander illustrates a scheme of causality which ignores the modern distinction between laws of nature and questions of justice: "The origin from which beings proceed is also the end towards which their destruction proceeds according to necessity; for they offer satisfaction and expiation to one another for their injustice according to the order of time."[63] The ancient scheme of rationalization which directly links suffering evil and doing evil preserves the holiness of the divine. If humankind suffers because of human impurity, then God remains innocent.

What endures in the transposition of the primary symbol of defilement as consciousness of the fault is the reference to a divine being who has a transcendent innocence. What changes with an increased human awareness of defilement is the rationalization of a primitive or naive consciousness for suffering evil. For instance, the figure of the suffering, just man represented by both a Babylonian and a Hebrew Job decisively shatters the immediate association of physical suffering with ethical evil. The symbolic structure of defilement is gradually transposed to constitute the symbolism of sin. Whereas defilement reflected a pre-ethical awareness of faulted existence, sin represents an ethical consciousness of being captive to evil.

Ricoeur stresses that the Babylonian confession of sins presents a most remarkable example of a transition from the symbolism of defilement to sin considered as the second primary symbol. It is the

---

[61] Ibid., p. 25.
[62] Ibid., p. 31.
[63] Ibid.; cf. Diels, *Fragment* B1.

relation to a personal God that determines the spiritual space according to which the consciousness of sin replaces that of defilement. The confession of sins introduces the feeling of being abandoned by one's God: "How long, O god, will you do this to me? I am treated as one who fears neither god nor goddess."[64] The initial moment of the awareness of sin presupposes a preliminary encounter with the divine that is lost by the penitent who suffers and fears the absence or silence of his or her God. The prior establishment of a covenant is seen in the Hebrew experience of sin.

Before describing the purest formulation of the experience of sin, Ricoeur explains that, according to evidence accumulated from the history of ancient religions,

> the cultures that were most advanced in meditation upon sin as a religious dimension "before God"—and, above all, the Hebrew culture never broke with the representation of defilement. The Levitical prescriptions, preserved in the Hebrew and Christian canon of the Bible, are evidence enough. Even if, as we believe, the intentions are different, and even opposed, they live together and sometimes contaminate one another to the point of becoming indistinguishable.[65]

This means that the different sets of primary intentions from the various ancient Western cultures, in their use of images such as defilement, do not prevent one culture's symbols contaminating symbolism of a different culture. To illustrate the elements of three other types of ancient myths can be found in the myth of Adam.[66] Ricoeur gives pre-eminence to the Adamic myth because, "by its complexity and its inner tensions, (it) reaffirms in varying degrees the essential truths of the other myths."[67]

In his essay on "Evil" Ricoeur clarifies this point:

> If we take the Adamic myth as a point of reference, we find in it the muted echo of all the others and vice versa. We can therefore speak of a tragic aspect in the Adamic myth, expressed in the deep and shadowy psychology of temptation. There is a sort of fatalistic side of the ethical confession of sins. But there is also, an irreducible remainder of the theogonic combat, which can be seen in the figure of the serpent and in other biblical figures

---

[64] Ibid., p. 49; cf. *Babylonian Penitential Psalms* (Oxford: Oxford University Press, 1927).

[65] Ibid., pp. 49–50.

[66] Ibid., pp. 306–46.

[67] Ibid., p. 309.

related to the primordial chaos. What is more, the essentially ethical affirmation of God's saintliness can never entirely rid us of the suspicion that God is somehow beyond good and evil and that for this very reason he sends evil as well as good...

The same thing should be said with respect to ...the Adamic myth and the myth of the exiled soul... The symbols of captivity and of exodus that underlie the Adamic myth...lend themselves to contamination by the symbolism, coming from another source, of a fallen "soul."[68]

It is important that the symbolism of sin does not simply replace the awareness of defilement. Ricoeur argues that the schemata of pardon and return, in particular, make intelligible the enduring aspect of defilement in the symbolism of sin.

Schemata need to be distinguished somehow from symbols. A schema, following Kant, is a temporal image which is used to determine a non-temporal concept or symbol; a symbol has, as defined earlier, a double intentionality which would also make them different from a schema. Of course Ricoeur seems to speak of schemata in pairs as with pardon and return.

The schema of pardon, for Ricoeur, renders meaningful both the symbol of sin's redemption and the symbol of defilement's purification. Pardon as a buying back—which is literally the meaning of redemption—mediates the meaning of sin as well as the more primitive meaning of defilement. The symbolism of redemption from sin and purification of defilement gravitates, according to Ricoeur, around the schemata of pardon and return. Return is, then, seen in the Judaeo-Christian myths to define sin retrospectively as a breaking of the covenant with God. The power which breaks this bond is like the substance-force of evil under the symbolism of defilement. This force makes it necessary for pardon to be a buying back, otherwise the human will is held captive.

The symbolism of redemption from sin is schematized by the biblical writers when they develop the meaning of the Exodus event. The Exodus is quite literally the buying back reflected in the actual going out or going up of Israel from Egypt. Ricoeur identifies the Exodus as the most significant cipher of the destiny of Israel.[69] At its extreme point the

---

[68] Ricoeur, "Evil," pp. 203–4.
[69] Ricoeur, *The Symbolism of Evil*, p. 92.

symbol of the Exodus as a buying back or pardoning is indistinguishable from the schema of going up or returning.[70]

Redemption is understood symbolically as the restoration of a covenant between God and humankind. This meaning of redemption is mediated by the biblical schemata of pardon and return. The schemata render the concept of redemption meaningful by providing "a schematism of analogy"[71] with sensible experience. It could be argued that the representative capacity of these schemata serves to mediate by means of analogy the antinomies of grace and free will, predestination and freedom.[72] The schema of pardon sometimes takes on the figurative form of a repentance of God, as if God changes his mind with regard to human beings (e.g. *Exodus* 32:14). This image of a repentant God does not imply that God actually changes but that the new restored relationship between God and humankind is divinely initiated. Pardon can also be imagined as the forgetting of the wrath of holiness.[73] These images of pardon need to be seen in relation to the correlative schema of return which also has several meanings. Return may signify the turning from an evil way.[74] It may also represent the renewal, by way of trust and quietness, of a primitive bond.[75] Images of return are further used in the manner of a conjugal metaphor which symbolizes the end of adultery and prostitution.[76]

Together pardon and return form a dialectical pair. It is not adequate simply to set the schemata of pardon and return in opposition to each other. Pardon is not simply what God does; neither is return strictly what human beings have to do. A straightforward correlation of pardon as God's act and return as a human action would render meaningless certain passages in the Judaeo-Christian scripture about the restoration of the covenant. For example, the Old Testament prophets both exhort the people to return, as if it depended entirely on humankind, yet at the same time implore the return as if it depended solely on God. In particular Jeremiah says, "Make me return and I shall return."[77] Ricoeur interprets the mythical narratives concerning redemption with regard to

---

[70] See *Isaiah* 51:9–10 and *Psalm* 89:10; in these verses Rahab serves as a poetical name for the Egypt of the Exodus.

[71] Ricoeur, "Freedom in the Light of Hope," p. 424n.

[72] Ibid; and *The Symbolism of Evil*, p. 81.

[73] Ricoeur, *The Symbolism of Evil*, p. 78.

[74] Cf. *Jeremiah*.

[75] *Isaiah* 30:15.

[76] Cf. *Hosea*.

[77] Ricoeur, *The Symbolism of Evil*, p.80; cf. *Jeremiah* 17:14.

this dialectical relationship between human and divine action and so stresses that human choice always involves a suspensive power. Consequently pardon appears conditional.[78]

Ricoeur describes the purest formulation of the experience of sin in terms of vocation and invocation. What appears in the first place is a modality of the divine presence in a commandment which represents an expression of a holy will and a human vocation. The Hebrew covenant (*Berit*) is based upon this idea of an original, divinely given vocation. The experience of sin is not initially the violation of an abstract rule, but the breaking of a personal bond. This means that before becoming a form of ethical transgression sin has a purely religious significance. Invocation arises, then, from the state of sin in which the loss of the bond between divine holiness and human goodness results in the loss of humankind's original vocation. What appears prior to sin is the human vocation. Invocation by the sinner reflects the possibility of the restoration of the human and divine covenant.

According to Ricoeur's symbolic account of sin, pardon and return come together in the historical celebrations of the Exodus.[79] God not only delivers from captivity but is able to redeem and purify humankind. The symbolism of sin is enriched retrospectively as Egypt becomes the cipher of captivity for the Hebrew people. Captivity is seen as the most powerful symbol of the human condition under the influence of evil.

> The captivity is literally a social, inter-subjective situation. In becoming the symbol of sin, this cipher displayed the alienating character of sin; the sinner is "in" the sin as the Hebrew was "in" bondage, and sin is thus an evil "in which" humankind is caught. That is why it can be at the same time personal and communal, transcending consciousness, known to God alone in its reality and its truth: that, too, is why it is a power that binds man (woman), hardens him (her), and holds him (her) captive; and it is this experience of the impotence of captivity that makes possible a taking over of the theme of defilement. However, "internal" to the heart of humankind the principle of this bondage may be, the bondage in fact constitutes an enveloping situation, like a snare in which humankind is caught; and so something of unclean contact is retained in this idea of the "captivity" of sin.[80]

Finally, the third of Ricoeur's primary symbols needs to be described. Guilt becomes the hyper-ethical awareness of doing evil; guilt occurs

---

[78] Cf. *Deuteronomy* 11:26–28, 30:15–19.

[79] Cf. *Isaiah* 44:21–23 and *Deuteronomy* 21:8.

[80] Ricoeur, *The Symbolism of Evil*, p. 93.

when the individual consciousness turns in on itself. In Ricoeur's words, "according to the schema of sin, evil is a situation 'in which' humankind is caught as a single collective; according to the schema of guilt, evil is an act that each individual 'begins.'"[81] Developing this contrast between guilt and sin he explains:

> The guilty conscience is shut in first of all because it is an isolated conscience that breaks the communion of sinners. It "separates" itself in the very act by which it takes upon itself, and upon itself alone, the whole weight of evil. The guilty conscience is shut in even more secretly by an obscure acquiescence in its evil, by which it make itself its own tormentor. It is in this sense that guilty conscience is a slave and not only consciousness of enslavement.[82]

Thus understood a guilty conscience does not involve an awareness of the possibility of deliverance. For Ricoeur, freedom and innocence can only be understood in relation to the second Adam and so according to the deliverance from sin's captivity. He points to three crucial characteristics of the symbolism of sin which need to be seen in relation to the second Adam who, as already found, represents innocent freedom.

First, the ontological dimension of sin presents the real situation of humankind. It is the heart—the very existence—of the human being that is evil, no matter what human consciousness of it may be. Second, sin is at once personal and communal. This second characteristic confirms the first characteristic of the reality of sin and also constitutes the condition which may be described as the captivity of sin. Third, the self-recognition of reality and captivity of sin is to be confessed in the absolute sight of an eternal, holy God. The proclamation of the Hebrew prophet Jeremiah encompasses these three characteristics according to an implicit motif of radical evil. The recognition of the condition that has been found to be, in Kantian terms, an inclination to evil inherent in human nature is essentially proclaimed by Jeremiah who is recorded as saying: "The heart of man is deceitful above all things and incurably evil: who can know it? I, the Eternal, search the heart and try the reins."[83] The eternal God who possesses an absolute sight and remains beyond the inconstant, corrupted human heart somehow still judges with mercy and compassion the passage of a temporal life as a unified whole. The idea of a holy, eternal will seems diametrically opposed to the fascinating,

---

[81] Ibid., pp. 106–7.
[82] Ibid., p. 146.
[83] *Jeremiah* 17:9–10.

binding, frenetic force described by the biblical writers as at the heart of the evil disposition. This force inevitably causes the separation, rebellion and going astray which constitutes the experience of sin. On what ground can humankind hope to be saved from a radical evil which, initially, is recognized as perverting the ground of all moral maxims but, gradually, manifests itself in the enveloping situation of sin? What sort of God would create such a situation and then expect the human creature to hope?

An attempt to scrutinize the Kantian theoretical question concerning the noumenal choice made in the face of a radical alternative between goodness and evil will not be given at this stage in the symbolic reconstruction of Ricoeur's account of human evil. Instead the concern will be with the practical problem and the symbolic expression of liberation as deliverance from the captivity that becomes manifest in social and self alienation. Moving beyond Kant's theoretical antinomies the symbolism of redemption from sin as represented by the second Adam may be restored, following Ricoeur, by recognising in practical terms the meaning of being captive.[84]

To be consistent with Ricoeur's dual-aspect account of experience captivity has to be conceived as the passivity of being affected by changing temporal conditions which become external and internal alienations, as well as the activity of being able to affect change which reflects a voluntary deviation from the good. Yet this means that the awareness of sin involves recognising the Kantian paradox of self-affection,[85] the experience of which gives rise to the symbolism of captivity, of social and self alienation, as well as of deliverance. The captivity which is sin arises within the fundamental dual-aspect structure of human experience and so the experience of sin cannot be expressed in unequivocal terms, but only in symbolic language. Events like the Exodus become symbols that reveal, as in rites of expiation or sacrifice, how the meaning of present personal and communal experience always includes the past and the future. The present symbolized event of sacrifice involves both memory and expectation. This is to say that memory of an original innocence, symbolically understood as being defiled in human experience by a stain, is intimately

---

[84] Ricoeur, *The Symbolism of Evil*, p. 93.

[85] Kant's paradox is recognized in the inexplicable fact that the awareness of our own states of consciousness as temporally (and spatially) represented, i.e. as affected, is the outcome of the non-temporal affecting by ourselves as we are in ourselves; cf. Kant, *Critique of Pure Reason*, B67–69, B156–57.

connected in the rite of sacrifice with the expectation of a restoration of that primordial innocence.

David Damrosh acknowledges that Ricoeur's interpretation of sacrifice, especially of *Leviticus* 17, in *The Symbolism of Evil* is a pioneering study.[86] We might agree that Ricoeur's critical restoration of biblical symbolism is significant for revealing the way in which pardon and return can be objectified in ceremonial expiation. Expiation is anticipated and recollected in the sacrifice of God in Christ. Ricoeur's reading of *Leviticus* represents sacrifice of an innocent victim in expiation as means to salvation.[87] It is true, however, that for Ricoeur *Leviticus* is not only about sacrifice; it is also concerned with the primary, enduring symbolism of defilement.[88]

As seen above the schemata of return and pardon reflect the enduring aspect of defilement—i.e. the substance-force—of evil from which there is a need for purification—sin the symbolism of sin. From the point of view of sin we see further that return is not strictly the act of humankind and pardon that of God. Similarly in *The Symbolism of Evil* expiation is not interpreted as the action of the human person alone who must make sacrifices. Ricoeur contends that in *Leviticus* 17:5–11 the priest in his performance of the expiatory rite does not have a magical hold over the divine. Neither is it strictly the role of the human agent to make expiation. Instead the symbolism of ceremonial expiation creates an analogical bond by which participation in a first level meaning gives rise to a second level of meaning.

As defined in *The Symbolism of Evil*, sympathetic re-enactment restores a first level of meaning to the rite of expiation. This more apparent meaning constitutes pardon as buying back which is itself intimately connected with return as repenting. The confession of sin

---

[86]   David Damrosh's chapter on *Leviticus*, in Robert Alter and Frank Kermode (eds), *Literary Guide to the Bible* (London: Collins, 1987), especially p. 76n4.

[87]   Ricoeur, *The Symbolism of Evil*, p. 98.

[88]   Julia Kristeva, although without any direct recognition, critically advances Ricoeur's textual analysis of sacrifice and defilement. According to Kristeva, sacrifice manifests a logic of separation, distribution, and difference; this logic is set up in the biblical text between purity/impurity, immortality/morality, and hence between human identity and the divine. Also defilement points to but does not signify an autonomous force which can be threatening for divine agency. Defilement serves in the logic of distribution, such as is seen in sacrificial rites of purification, upon which a symbolic community is founded. See Kristeva, *Powers of Horror: An Essay on Abjection*, trans. Leon Roudiez (New York: Columbia University Press, 1982), pp. 90–113.

gives rise to a second level of meaning. Especially noteworthy is that the symbolism of blood in the rite points to the mediating function of the sacrificial figure in the redemption from sin. The blood itself symbolizes the gift or offering of life which refers to a vital continuity between the offering and the man or woman who presents the offering; it refers as well to the gift of a restored relationship between humankind and God.[89] The action of expiation in this interpretation is made by the person through his or her gift in the sacrifice.

The very same action may be reinterpreted so that the emphasis is placed upon God's gift of the means of expiation—upon the words "I have given it to you, upon the altar, in order that..."[90] Here the priest who makes expiation becomes the performer of a mystery, the meaning of which is given by God through the blood and the offering of life. Neither of these interpretations—the one emphasising the human action and the other stressing divine action—considers the death of the victim as an act of punitive justice, rather it is a symbolic offering of life which carries a double meaning.[91] Yet this second interpretation gives to the Hebrew sacrifice a meaning favorable to what has by retroaction a christological significance: to emphasize that God gives the means of expiation is to say that He pardons and so make expiation a means to pardon.[92]

The crucial thing for Ricoeur is that expiation and pardon appear as one in the sacrifice of Christ who is both the gift of God and the gift of human life. In this way the second Adam restoration of an innocent freedom constitutes the gift of regeneration. Human evil is understood retrospectively: while the type of regeneration represents an original innocence, the anti-type, which represents the generation of sin, is understood to be the temporal condition of a dual-aspect being. Sin can be interpreted retrospectively as the ontological condition of human willing. But the gift of transcendence is only fully disclosed, for Ricoeur,

---

[89] Ibid., pp. 96–101; here Kristeva offers a reading of the blood in relation to the symbolic order as a place for abjection. Kristeva defines abjection as refusal of the defiling, impure, uncontrollable materiality of a subject's embodied existence; the abject is a condition of the unified subject, yet is intolerable to that subject.

[90] *Leviticus* 17:11.

[91] Kristeva recognizes in sacrifice a specific relation between purity/impurity which pertains to setting in order; this relation is not an absolute opposition but it is inscribed in the biblical text and it constitues the strict identities of human/divine. In turn these identities are held together by expulsion of the abject. See *Powers of Horror*, pp. 95–99; also my "Ricoeur and Hick on Evil."

[92] Ricoeur, *The Symbolism of Evil*, pp. 21–22, 99.

by the eschatological figure of hope whose gift of life reveals that divine innocence and freedom are yet more fundamental for the dual-aspect being than human guilt and the captivity which constitutes sin.

IV. Symbolic Reconstruction and Truth

Crucial for the intellectual legitimation of the representations of sin and of grace in the symbolism of sacrifice is Ricoeur's reconstruction of the deeply ambiguous nature of the experience of being captive as dual-aspect beings. But why should the symbolic reconstruction of the first and second Adam be constituted according to a post-Kantian philosophical anthropology? We could answer that Kant's dual-aspect account of human experience makes intelligible the symbolism of *un libre arbitre captif.* Yet the more adequate answer to this question is simply that Ricoeur's post-Kantian account of human willing both is informed by and informs Judaeo-Christian symbolism. Also that the restored myths of innocence, the fall, and salvation are given priority over questions of Christ's historicity follows from Kant's insistence on the practical usefulness of Christian symbolism.

If human nature is understood to be ideally represented in the schematization of the archetype, then the truth and meaning of sin and grace may be thought to be schematized by the myths of the first and second Adam. The myths which arise out of the experience of a captive free will provide the symbolism for sin, as well as for the deliverance from captivity. In addition the symbolic narratives constituting these myths manifest a human capacity to reconstruct as an intelligible totality—i.e. to symbolize according to a narrative plot—not only both the individual and the universal but also the contrast between time and eternity.

Especially significant in the symbolism of captivity and deliverance is the transformative power represented by the narratives concerning the incarnate life of Christ. The power to transform human consciousness and circumstances depends upon the constitutive role of narrative activity in actual historical experience. For Ricoeur it is the historical experience of Christ's life, death, and resurrection which can be narrativized and symbolically re-enacted. The myth of the second Adam and the ritual interpretation of Christ's sacrifice, when expressed and celebrated in definite tradition-determined ways, serve as further specifications of the transforming power of the divine incarnation.[93]

In a similar manner but without the uniqueness assigned to the sacrifice of Christ, such ritual celebrations of sacrifice as found in *Leviticus* 17 have always developed in response to natural events and have become embedded in religious traditions. This means that the relationship between the human and divine is not only symbolized by the myths of the first and second Adam. Yet what precisely constitutes for Ricoeur the truth of these symbolic reconstructions? That Christ is conceived to have been a particular historical individual who, by the grace of the mythico-poetic imagination, equally symbolizes the universal meaning and experiences of humankind as dual-aspect beings may not be enough to establish this as a true narrative account of the life, death and resurrection of the innocent God-man, Jesus Christ.

Questions concerning the truth of the revelatory symbol remain without definite answers at the end of this chapter. What, it may be asked, makes the figure of hope more than an idol, a wish-fulfilment or an illusion constituted out of a human need for protection from the harshness of reality? These questions may create great difficulties for Ricoeur's symbolic reconstruction. Yet I find significance, for instance, in René Girard's view. Girard supports Ricoeur by, on the one hand, offering criticisms of Christianity generally yet, on the other hand, praising Ricoeur's dual hermeneutics of Christian symbolism.

In *Things Hidden Since the Foundation of the World*, Girard argues persuasively against the whole sacrificial interpretation of Christianity, as well as against those who maintain an anti-Christian position but who still reinforce Christian notions of sacrifice. Girard maintains that the re-enactment of Christ's death in the Christian eucharist should expose the violence and illusion of the sacrificial process, since Christ as "the victim is declared innocent of the evil of which the victim is accused (in the traditional sacrificial rites)."[94] His argument is that Christ's act reveals the religious illusion—and, by contrast, authentic love—by uncovering the hidden mechanism of the scapegoat which characterizes a community's performance of ritual sacrifice and, more broadly, the violence of culture. For Girard, a non-sacrificial reading of the eucharist

---

[93] Ibid., pp. 94–99.

[94] René Girard, *Violence and the Sacred*, trans. Patrick Gregory (Baltimore: The Johns Hopkins University Press, 1977), especially chapter 4, "The Origin of Myth and Ritual," pp. 89–118; and *Things Hidden Since the Foundation of the World*, trans. Stephen Bann (Books II and III) and Michael Metteer (Book I) (London: Athlone, 1987).

should serve as an ideology critique of culture and religion. Yet Girard does not immediately condemn the sacrificial reading of Christianity precisely because rites of sacrifice in fact developed in order to protect humankind from violence. Before humankind can be completely free from the myths, rites, and taboos that constitute the religious foundation of culture the danger of violence against which they have served historically to protect us must be understood.

At the same time Girard contends that Ricoeur's critical and restorative hermeneutics of the symbolism concerning Christ's sacrifice holds an extremely important place in the mediation of belief and modern criticism of such belief. He claims that Ricoeur is one contemporary philosopher who "is willing to argue with determination that both positions are necessary."[95] Ricoeur argues both for a hermeneutics of faith which supports the sacrificial reading of religion and a hermeneutics of suspicion which should challenge and unmask the violence that, as Girard argues, lies behind the victim mechanism. Granted Ricoeur's hermeneutics of suspicion, he significantly aims to uncover the power of evil that undermines human freedom and responsibility.

My conclusion is that Ricoeur himself poses the most radical questions for his own position. This is said in full knowledge of both contemporary interpretations of religious belief and philosophical problems related to the intellectual legitimation of that belief. Ricoeur calls into question the very presuppositions of his Judaeo-Christian faith by endeavoring to confront the critiques of religion put forth by Marx, Nietzsche, and Freud. It is such confrontation which enables me in the concluding chapter to begin to disentangle the concrete possibilities of Ricoeur's project from its mystifying elements.

---

[95] Girard, *Things Hidden*, p. 445.

Kant... is without a doubt the philosopher who has
never ceased to inspire me...
the philosopher who joins a precise architectonic of
the power of thought to
an intransigent sense of the limits

Ricoeur 1978

Conclusion

I have endeavored to reconstruct Paul Ricoeur's philosophy of the will in order to assess critically its contribution to post-Kantian debates. My critical restoration has been called for because Ricoeur has not completed the projected work of constructing a philosophy of the will; nor has he discussed the theological assumptions of his project. In concluding I intend to stress the ways in which the exegetical, critical, and restorative aims of the preceding chapters develop a Kantian reading of Ricoeur's project which has timely significance for modernity and postmodernity.[1]

The exegetical aim of this interpretative study has been to expose and assemble the diverse elements of Ricoeur's philosophy of the will in a manner which makes his earliest work accessible to philosophers and theologians. We have seen that Ricoeur has completed two volumes on the will—*Freedom and Nature* and *Finitude and Guilt*. As set out in the introduction to the first of these works, his project was also to include a volume on the poetics of willing but this has never been written. However, many of the articles and books which Ricoeur has written since 1950, when *Le volontaire et l'involontaire* (the original French edition of *Freedom and Nature*) is first published, have taken up themes concerning the will. Not only have questions concerning human freedom, evil and hope been central to Ricoeur's continuing project but, more recently, his writings have been concerned with the possibility of a poetics. Clearly the diversity of ideas which comprise Ricoeur's philosophy of the will have emerged in answer to quite different questions and have developed out of various concerns such as the relation of human freedom to nature, and the possibility and actuality of evil. These concerns initially led Ricoeur to develop an eidetics, empirics, mythics, and hermeneutics of the will.

A major critical aim in my interpretation of Ricoeur has been to analyze the Kantian problematic which informs his thinking. I have

---

[1] See my "A Question of Personal Identity."

attempted to follow Ricoeur by endeavoring to be a child of criticism. In his words,

> we are in every way children of criticism, and we seek to go beyond criticism by means of criticism, by a criticism that is no longer reductive but restorative.[2]

Accordingly, in addition to the exegetical and critical aims, there is a dimension of my work which endeavors to extend Ricoeur's philosophy by developing his restorative criticism.

The potentiality of Ricoeur's restorative criticism can be usefully compared with Walter Benjamin's redemptive or rescuing criticism (*Rettungskritik*). Benjamin uses the image of a wizened, ugly hunchback to represent the redemptive—yet discredited, shameful and so hidden— service of theology in modern times.[3] This image of the hidden significance of a redemptive task which is portrayed by Benjamin can help to encapsulate the latent meaning of Ricoeur's emphasis upon the re-enactment and possible regeneration of the past in the avowal of evil and consciousness of fault. To recall a passage from the Preface to *Fallible Man*, redemptive or restorative criticism brings the past and future together in present consciousness:

> The profound unity of the two temporal "ecstasies" (*extases*) of the past and the future appears primarily in the consciousness of fault. The forward *élan* of the project becomes overlaid with retrospection, while the distressed, remorseful contemplation of the past is combined with the certitude of possible regeneration; the project, enriched by memory, re-emerges as repentance. And so in the consciousness of fault, the future attempts to encompass the past, self-discovery shows itself as a recovery, and consciousness uncovers in itself a thickness or density which would not be recognized by a reflection attentive only to the forward *élan* of the project.[4]

This profound unity of the past and the future in the present awareness of the fault is not merely the recognition of an individual consciousness turned in on itself (which is the description given of the

---

[2] Ricoeur, *The Symbolism of Evil*, p. 350.

[3] Walter Benjamin, "Theses on the Philosophy of History," in Hannah Arendt (ed.), *Illuminations*, trans. Harry Zohn (London: Collins Fontana, 1973), pp. 254–60; see Thesis I, as well as Theses VI and IX. On affinity between Ricoeur's restorative criticism and Walter Benjamin's rescuing criticism (*Rettungskritik*) see Geoffrey Hartman, *Criticism in the Wilderness: The Study of Literature Today* (New Haven: Yale University Press, 1980), pp. 42–44, 63–85, 267–68.

[4] Ricoeur, *Fallible Man*, p. xxvi–xxvii.

modern consciousness of guilt in chapter three). Instead this is the basis for the potentially transformative project of humankind's effort and desire to be.[5] The passage just quoted reveals that, for Ricoeur, critical reflection in its very negativity—e.g. in its recognition of distress, remorse and its avowal of evil—becomes a mode of discovery leading to the restoration of innocence. Furthermore in order to uncover a primordial bond with the sacred, Ricoeur transcends critical thought insofar as this thought involves a forgetfulness of the sacred.[6]

Important is that Ricoeur chooses to develop a critical hermeneutics over and against a claim to absolute knowledge. This means he faces a potentially endless task of interpretation. We have seen that a conflict of interpretations marks his discussions concerning the meaning and application of the concepts of free will, original sin, and kingdom of God. Also Ricoeur acknowledges that there can be no absolute resolution of the conflict over the meaning of these fundamental concepts.

However there exists a problem for Ricoeur with an endless conflict of interpretations. This can be understood when his hermeneutics is placed along side a more radical view of critical hermeneutics. Geoffrey Hartman, for one, argues the case for a reflective hermeneutics in which the will must be actively mediating. It is worth quoting Hartman's view as applied to the dilemma of two types of modern society:

> The reflective person has to avoid being a mere reflex of others; a bundle of inherited intentions, a mediated rather than mediating will. The paradox is clear enough...
> Hermeneutics is an art that grows out of perplexity, out of finding an enigma where we expected a kerygma. Evidence fails or is disabled, and unusual or ungovernable types of interpretation come into play...
> No wonder some are scared witless by a mode of thinking that seems to offer no decidability, no resolution. Yet the perplexity that [hermeneutics] ... arouses in careful readers and viewers is hardly licentious. It is the reality; it is only as strange as truth... It recalls the prevalence of propaganda, both in open societies that depend on conversation, jawboning, advertizing, bargaining, and in controlled societies that can become sinister and inquisitorial, adding to their torture chamber the subtlest brainwashing and conditioning devices without giving up the brazen and

---

[5] Cf. Jean Nabert, *Elements of an Ethic*, pp. 14–15, 87–99, 115ff, 194; and Pierre Colin, "L'héritage de Jean Nabert," *Esprit: Changer la culture et la politique, tomes* 7–8, no. 140–41 (juillet-août 1988), pp. 119–28.

[6] Ricoeur, *The Symbolism of Evil*, p. 362.

reiterated lie. Can any hermeneutics... withstand either society while they are still distinguishable?[7]

The question is: How can the statement that modern hermeneutics grows out of finding an enigma where we expected a kerygma be reconciled with what Ricoeur calls a kerygma of love? In reading Freud Ricoeur claims that

> The only thing that can escape Freud's critique is faith as the kerygma of love: "God so loved the world..." But in return his critique can help me discern what this kerygma of love excludes—a penal Christology and a moral God—and what it implies—a certain coincidence of the tragic God of Job and the lyric God of John.[8]

But this kerygma seems to be little more than a dogma. Can it be established that Ricoeur's kerygma of love in some sense remains an enigma—if this is not a contradiction in terms—and that love has its source in an unfulfilled ontology of humankind's desire to be? This would preserve both an undecidability and a deferral of meaning. If these cannot be preserved, then can Ricoeur consistently claim the endless task of hermeneutics?

It is my claim that a more radical reconstruction of Ricoeur's hermeneutics can be potentially achieved by confronting concrete concerns. This would be radical in Hartman's terms of finding an enigma instead of a kerygma. We can then confront what Hartman calls the lie of modern societies as well as other forms of false consciousness by recalling certain points already made. For instance, the remarks on praxis at the end of chapter two draw attention to Ricoeur's socially significant insight concerning the cognitive power of narrative reconstructions. Of course here again Ricoeur's Kantian problematic confronts us with possible contradiction. To explain these remarks let us retrace some of our steps.

It was demonstrated in chapter one that Kant, in his critique of transcendental illusion, foreshadows the modern critiques of false consciousness formulated by the three masters, Marx, Nietzsche, and Freud. In this way Kant supports Ricoeur's hermeneutics of suspicion. Kant's critique of self-knowledge also supports the dual process of Ricoeur's positive and negative hermeneutics. In fact Ricoeur claims that

---

[7] Hartman, *Criticism in the Wilderness*, pp. 282–83.
[8] Ricoeur, *Freud and Philosophy*, p. 536.

critical hermeneutics is necessarily Kantian; and he admits the continuing influence of Kant:

> Kant...is without a doubt the philosopher who has never ceased to inspire me and to provoke me. I have always recognized in him the philosopher who joins a precise architectonic of the power of thought to an intransigent sense of the limits involved. When I started off along the path of symbolical interpretation, it was in Kant that I found the suggestion of uniting the investigation of schematism, hence of productive imagination, with the elaboration of limiting concepts, that is, of concepts which at once express the work of reason beyond understanding and prevent understanding from locking sense within fixed and closed determinations.[9]

In chapter two we saw that Kant's transcendental idealism provides a cognitive background for Ricoeur's concepts of freedom, temporality/non-temporality, and the mediating archetype of humankind. Yet the post-Kantian problematic which underlies and informs Ricoeur's thought has to be criticized. My central criticism is that the field of concepts and issues, which comprise Ricoeur's dual-aspect account of willing, relies upon an inevitably paradoxical account of the human subject as being temporal and non-temporal. A decisive problem emerges in trying to make sense of the contradictory idea of non-temporal activity. Yet some such activity had to be assumed if Ricoeur's schematization of the good principle in the archetype and, even more fundamental, Kant's synthetic activity of the pure concepts of understanding were to be accepted as cogent endeavors.

These abstract problems aside, chapter three emphasizes that a dialectical relationship between Ricoeur's philosophical anthropology and theology provides the framework for reconstructing his christology. Elaboration of this relationship reveals that Ricoeur's christology takes him beyond Kant's ahistorical references to Jesus Christ. Based upon the human bond with the sacred, Ricoeur's christology is paradigmatically represented by the myths of the first and second Adam. Yet, in the very same moment, Ricoeur maintains the actual historical uniqueness of Christ's life, death, and resurrection.[10]

Finally, in order to disentangle the less mystifying aspects of this reconstruction from the transcendental idealist problematic, let us return to certain concrete concerns. I assume that it is possible not to try to eliminate the paradoxical aspects of transcendental idealism, yet still try

---

[9] Ricoeur, "My Relation to the History of Philosophy," *Iliff Review* 35 (1978), p. 8.
[10] Cf. *The Symbolism of Evil*, pp. 269ff.

to find practical and symbolic significance in a post-Kantian account of experience.[11] The task is to emphasize the primacy of concrete dimensions of meaning.

From the outset of this book I have emphasized that Ricoeur's philosophical anthropology points to the religious dimension of human experience. It is my particular concern to recognize this dimension as a radical style of a comprehensive praxis.[12] We have also seen that Ricoeur interprets human experience according to the symbolism of captivity. What needs to be found is a definite methodology for the deliverance of experience from what is symbolically described as captivity, e.g. from oppression. For instance, consider the possibility of an authenticating faith. This faith would both constitute and be constituted by a continual process of authentication which, in turn, would reconstitute experience. In this way Ricoeur's philosophical anthropology may offer the possibility for praxis which transforms the world. Appropriately John O'Malley explains such faith as:

> a transcendental intuition in process of fulfilment, which, in that process, strives to transform the world in accordance with the project its *praxis*...seeks to embody effectively so that, apt carrier of the meaning so conferred upon and realized in it, this latter may there be transparently and fully manifest... Faith, it is true, may not and in practice, never can, rest quite assured of the absolute authenticity of its actual specification of its radically comprehensive project in its theoretic or pragmatic realization. It nonetheless remains *authenticating* in its continual awareness of this possibility and in its persisting patience to—as well as attentiveness to the exigency of—its critical reconstitution.[13]

Informed by this description of faith we can begin to see the concrete implications of the critical process constituted by Ricoeur's hermeneutics of faith and of suspicion.

Faith can only be authenticating if it discovers a reality that does not simply allow the suffering of marginalized others to become an already superseded fact of the past. Ricoeur takes what he conceives to be the Judaeo-Christian liberating memory as a paradigm. Although the most basic feature of a distinctively Jewish conception of experience is the experience of liberation that is portrayed in the Old Testament account of

---

[11]   Johann Baptist Metz, *Faith in History and Society*, trans. David Smith (Tunbridge Wells, Kent: Burns and Oats, 1980), pp. 17, 22–23, 52–51.

[12]   Cf. John O'Malley, *Sociology of Meaning* (London: Human Context Books, 1972), pp. 131, 134, 271.

[13]   Ibid., pp. 255–57.

the Exodus, Jesus Christ represents the radicalization of this Old Testament experience. In other words, Jesus Christ presents a decisive challenge concerning how the reality of God is to be understood and remembered in the face of the death of the other. It might be said that Christ as represented in the New Testament parables brings into question the social construction of reality.

Ricoeur has stressed the undeniable importance of Kant's practical reason in his philosophy of the will. Moreover Ricoeur's possible contribution to a theory of subjects, society, and history is reinforced by his *Lectures on Ideology and Utopia*, especially by the critical lectures on Jürgen Habermas (which reflect Ricoeur's own post-Hegelian Kantian standpoint); and more recently reinforced by his Gifford Lectures, *Oneself as Another*, especially the lecture on the self and the moral norm.[14] It is not within the scope of the present book to scrutinize these lectures. Yet for us it is absolutely significant that Ricoeur's works find the authentic foundation and limitation of his thought in Kant's practical philosophy.

We have found that Ricoeur could only speak of God in the context of the freedom of human persons and so in a post-Hegelian Kantian context in which reason becomes practical. God could only be a reality for human subjects who act freely, but as objects of thought neither the self nor God can be known in themselves. The primacy of practical over theoretical reason means that the goal of discourse about God is intended to be liberating, transforming action. The interaction of subjects is a temporal, creative, and innovative process, whereby freely willing agents surpass strictly determining conditions and define their own world and a common world. This interaction constitutes the condition of possibility of the identity of human subjects. In this context, we might not even need to postulate an ontologically distinct, transcendental subject as the universal condition for the identity of particular subjects. Might the identity of subjects, then, depend upon a post-Hegelian mutual recognition and interaction of free subjects? This could be something like what is sketched in the "Post-Hegelian Kantian Standpoint" section of chapter two.

The postmodern critique which culminates with a decentered subject is challenged by Ricoeur who insists upon the possibility of recentered and recentering subjects.[15] This means a human subject is constituted

---

[14] See Ricoeur, "Eighth Study: The Self and the Moral Norm," *Oneself as Another*, pp. 205–18; also 220–26, 238–39; "Huitième étude. Le soi et la norme morale, 1. La visée de la 'vie bonne' et l'obligation," *Soi-même comme un autre*, pp. 239–54; also 257–63, 276–78.

[15] Ricoeur, *Freud and Philosophy*, pp. 422, 462ff; and *Time and Narrative*, III, p. 217ff.

by and constitutes self-identity in recognition of the self as an other.[16] This dialectical understanding of human subjects depends not only upon a theory of social relations which prevents overly abstract thought but a theory of history which faces up to the experience of the death of the other.

To explain, the possibility of the identity of subjects as free agents resides in the radicality with which the other is affirmed; and this affirmation is, in turn, the basic practical demand in terms of which the complex social structure of any society is to be measured. A basic suspicion which underlies the modern critique of religion arises from the illusory projection of the individual subject who seeks to secure and stabilize his or her own actions. To avoid this an adequate dialectical theory of history is, as we will conclude, also crucial.

We have seen in discussion of his post-Hegelian Kantianism that Ricoeur stresses the significance of Kant's dialectic of practical reason, as well as his postulates of human freedom and of the existence of God. This Kantian emphasis enables Ricoeur to define the will in the light of hope for a practical realization of the highest good.[17] One crucial argument is as follows:

> What does the dialectic of practical reason add that is new? Essentially a transposition to the will of what we might call the completion structure of pure reason… What [the dialectic of practical reason] does give to our will is essentially a *goal—die Absicht aufs hîchste Gut*. That goal is the expression, on the level of duty, of the demand, the claim—the *Verlangen*—which constitutes pure reason in its speculative and practical use; reason "demands the absolute totality of conditions for a given conditioned thing" (beginning of the Dialectic of the *Critique of Practical Reason*)… What the will thus requires, Kant calls "the entire object of pure practical reason." …the concept of the highest good is both purified of all speculation by the critique of the transcendental illusion and entirely measured by the problematic of practical reason, that is, of the will.
>
> …the postulate of the existence of God… is "the adequate cause of this effect which is manifested to our will as its entire object, namely, the highest good." What is postulated is the *Zusammenhang*, the connection, in a being who encompasses the principle of accord between the two constituents of the highest good. But the postulate holds only insofar as we will, from the depths of our will, that the highest good be realized.[18]

---

16 Ricoeur, *Soi-même comme un autre*, pp. 14ff, 406–9; *Oneself as Another*, pp. 3f, 353.
17 Ricoeur, "Freedom in the Light of Hope," pp. 415–21.
18 Ibid., pp. 416, 421.

This recalls points concerning the highest good and the entire object of our will made in chapter two. To understand the way in which the will aims to realize the highest good it is necessary to project Ricoeur's poetics. The poetics should offer the greatest possibilities for the restoration and transformation of human/divine knowledge into a comprehensive style of praxis.

The word poetic is associated with the transformation of reason and desire whereby human willing engages in creative forms of praxis.[19] Essentially Ricoeur's poetics of the will would constitute the possibility of a new narrative description of reality, a reinterpretation which aims to change the world, and a revelation that transforms self-deception into increased understanding. To give definition to Ricoeur's projected poetics consider the threefold distinction of a naive, a historical, and a salvational poetics.

First, a naive poetics would assert the immediate and exclusive presence of the sensory dimension of poetry. This ignores what is in Kantian terms the mediating role of the productive imagination. Second, a historical poetics would exist only in a scattered form and promises nothing except that poetic thought will continue to become. A truly historical poetics would attempt to think in a strictly temporal dimension. Third, a salvational poetics would endeavor to conquer the timeless by way of a return to origins. Salvational criticism has a mythico-poetic concern in that although caught in time, in virtue of the fact that it is practiced as a discipline of thought, it turns to primordial origins in order to escape the emptiness and impoverishment of historical reality. In the words of Philip Wheelwright, a representative of salvational poetics:

> The ground-base of poetic truth is the truth, contextual but real, of man's possible redemption through the fullest imaginative response.[20]

Ricoeur's claims for a poetics of the will seem to have the greatest affinity with a salvational poetics. His hermeneutics of symbol and myth reflects the essence of a poetics in which, according to Paul de Man, "originary beginnings take on the appearance of privileged moments beyond time, and their remembrance serves as the promise of a

---

[19] For instance *mimesis* as discussed above.

[20] Philip Wheelwright, *The Burning Fountain* (Bloomington: Indiana University Press, 1954), p. 302.

new fruitfulness."[21] For salvational poetics history, conceived as being the dimension of temporal necessity, is conquered by the imagination of a possible redemption. However, once more there arises the problem of a paradox constituted by opposing temporal conditions to primordial origins which, supposedly, are grasped by the non-temporal activity of the imagination. The question that needs to be formulated, then, is how can the paradox which seems to constitute the essence of such a poetics be reconciled with the belief in a poetics that constitutes a salvational act capable of transcending the dilemma of temporality and non-temporality?[22]

Ricoeur's hope of answering this question rests in developing his concept of praxis.[23] The reason for having devoted so much attention to Ricoeur's ultimately paradoxical account of human willing is that this background becomes essential for understanding precisely the dilemmas which need to be overcome by a radical style of a comprehensive praxis. Let me very briefly mention the historico-philosophical background to the term praxis in the western intellectual tradition.

The Greek word praxis ordinarily means action or doing. However the philosophy of Aristotle establishes an important contrast between *praxis* and *theoria*. The former term designates the activities characteristic of man's ethical and political life while the latter term signifies those activities that are concerned with knowing for its own sake. In modern times it is the followers of Hegel who give a further significance to praxis. In their endeavor to go beyond Hegel his followers aim to transform social life and define praxis as the goal of developing the future in the realm of concrete activity.[24] In particular Marx, in the eighth of his "Theses on Feuerbach," goes so far as to claim that

---

[21] Paul De Man, *Blindness and Insight: Essays in the Rhetoric of Contemporary Criticism*, second edn (London: Methuen, 1983), p. 242.

[22] Cf. David Jasper, "The Limits of Formalism and The Theology of Hope: Ricoeur, Moltmann and Dostoyevsky," *Literature and Theology*, vol. 1, no.1 (March 1987), p. 6ff.

[23] Cf. Ricoeur, "The Teleological and Deontological Structures of Action: Aristotle and/or Kant?" in A. Phillips Griffiths (ed.), *Contemporary French Philosophy* (Cambridge: Cambridge University Press, 1987), pp. 99–111.

[24] See Nicholas Lobkowicz, *Theory and Practice: History of a Concept from Aristotle to Marx* (Notre Dame: University of Notre Dame Press, 1967); David McLellan, *The Young Hegelians and Karl Marx* (London: Macmillan, 1969), p. 10; and Ricoeur, "From Marxism to Contemporary Communism," in David Stewart and J. Bien (eds), *Political and Social Essays* (Athens: Ohio University Press, 1974), p. 220ff.

all social life is essentially *practical*. All mystery which leads theory to mysticism find their rational solution in historical practice and in the comprehension of this practice.[25]

Amending slightly Marx's claim, it can be said that there is also an expressive aspect that is constitutive of human personal and social being. The really significant advance Marx makes concerning the transformation of human praxis is that he connects praxis with action that aims at fundamentally radical political change. Finally, *Time and Narrative* identifies three modes of praxis, i.e. *mimesis*$_{1-3}$. These can be understood in the light of the above sketch of the philosophical development of the term.

Ricoeur defines a first mode of praxis as narrative prefiguration. Prefiguration refers to the pre-understanding which is necessary in the constitution of everyday practical knowledge. Configuration, as a second mode of praxis, stands for the synthesizing activity by which the knowledge of action is made the object of a conscious and systematic unity, e.g. the organized plot of a literary or historical narrative. Ricoeur calls a third mode of praxis transfiguration or, as he also refers to it, refiguration. Understood with reference to a social, literary, or historical text the agent of a transfiguration is the reader. The important element of this last mode of praxis is the possibility of going beyond (trans— meaning beyond) figuration or of giving form again (re—signifying again). For Ricoeur praxis as especially evident in the narrative constructions which are made possible by these three modes of figuration involves both an expressive and a practical aspect.[26]

In addition, a recent emphasis upon praxis by theologians who appropriate the Marxist critiques of the Frankfurt School philosophers partially informs Ricoeur's view of praxis and poetics. At least Johann Baptist Metz stresses for Ricoeur the role of community in the critique of ideology and the rediscovery of solidarity in the dangerous liberating memory of its narratives.[27]

Ricoeur, in developing a philosophy of the will, may not have initially set out to create a new perspective on human praxis, especially with regard to its social, political and religious dimensions. Nevertheless his original concern with the will, freedom, and the symbolism of

---

[25] Karl Marx and Friedrich Engels, *Collected Works*, vol 5 (London: Lawrence and Wishart, 1976), p. 5.

[26] Ricoeur, *Time and Narrative*, I, pp. 52–57; III, pp. 11, 159, 326.

[27] Ricoeur expresses his debt to Johann Baptist Metz's political theology in his unpublished Sarum Lectures on "Narrative Theology" (Oxford 1980).

captivity means that, right from the beginning of his formative project, there are the seeds for generating a perspective on responsible action and a transformation of restrictive praxis. Human freedom could not be understood without considering the deliverance of experience which is lived by beings who recognize themselves as being captive. And, for Ricoeur, the reality which constitutes the hope for such deliverance is conceived to be the God portrayed in the narrative accounts about the life, death, and resurrection of Jesus Christ. Equally Ricoeur stresses that God can only be understood in the context of the freedom of human subjects. It follows that his philosophy of the will provides the grounds for a critique of an individualistic and mystifying interpretation of tradition but, as it has been seen in this study, his criticism remains essentially a restorative criticism. This means that Ricoeur does not dispute the very possibility of theology. He endeavors to restore the authentic practical context—i.e. a transformed human consciousness as well as changed social and political circumstances—in which human beings may freely become responsible subjects and may hope for the deliverance of all humankind.

It is, I maintain, germane to reiterate that a poetics of the will is nowhere to be found in a single volume by Ricoeur. However his projected poetics remains important to his claims concerning a hermeneutical theology which endeavors to preserve a dialectic between political praxis and textual poetics. He distinguishes this from a political theology. In Ricoeur's words:

> I do not think that...we may substitute a political theology for a hermeneutical one... I hold...that a hermeneutics that takes the world of the text as its central category does not run the risk of privileging the dialogical relation between author and the reader, nor any personal decision in the face of the text. The amplitude of the world of the text requires an equal amplitude on the side of the *applicatio*, which will be as much political praxis as the labor of thought and language.
>
> ...If I have so sought to preserve the poetic qualification of the naming of God, it is to preserve the precious dialectic of poetics and politics. Certainly, human existence is political existence. Yet the texts within which Christian existence understands itself are not political to the extent that they are poetical.[28]

The stress on the poetical over the political means that praxis has to be understood, for Ricoeur, as not strictly political and practical but

---

[28] Ricoeur, "Naming God," p. 227.

also—and more significantly—as symbolic and expressive in its power to transform human self-consciousness and concrete circumstances. Poetic is used in this context by Ricoeur as an adjective which characterizes the narrative text as opening up a new world. This poetics of narrativity offers, to reiterate, a redescription of reality and a potentiality for transforming the human will in and through new forms of praxis.

It is as well to be critical of Ricoeur's poetics of narrativity. In fact *Time and Narrative*, III stresses that the problem for the refiguration of human time is the confrontation between the aporia of temporality and the poetics of narrativity.[29] We might suggest a re-assessment of the mythico-poetic imagination in its mimetic activity.[30] This activity of narrative construction is supposed to constitute an intelligible whole which is both a communal work and a dynamic praxis.[31] Yet major criticism regarding the mimetic activity is that there exists no guarantee on the validity and the authority of cognitive categories such as the pure productive *a priori* imagination. Here I insist, especially, upon scrutinizing the social and cultural agents who are responsible for the symbolic constitution of mythical narratives.[32]

The fundamental problem is that Ricoeur's mythico-poetic conception of the imagination depends upon a paradoxical conception of the human subject as dual agent. It is not clear whether or not Ricoeur simply assumes an *epistemological* distinction between the empirical and intelligible characters of the one rational agent. In fact the subject also seems to be split *ontologically* into both a concrete, desiring agent and an abstract, non-specific rational agent. But, then, who (or what) is given the responsibility for narrative constructions? If we assume an ontological split—no matter the epistemological reading—how do we make concrete sense of an abstract, non-specific agent or transcendental subject? A practical consequence of giving the responsibility of narrative constructions to an abstract subject would be the difficulty of preventing interpretative narratives from remaining blind to differences of gender, race, class, and ethnicity. Would the narratives of such an abstract subject only represent the biases of the dominant tradition?

A related difficulty with Ricoeur's enterprise of restoring an authentic meaning to Kantian tradition is his *refusal*, at one and the same

---

[29] Ricoeur, *Time and Narrative*, III, pp. 99–103, 270.

[30] See my "Paul Ricoeur on Narrative Identity and the Mythico-Poetic Imagination."

[31] Ricoeur, *Time and Narrative*, I, pp. 52–87.

[32] Ricoeur, *The Symbolism of Evil*, p. 166.

time, of a strictly autonomous conception of the human self and of an ideology of individualism both of which, nevertheless, are often thought to have been presupposed by Kant's philosophy. With regard to this difficulty, Metz proposes that modern theologians have differed radically according to their respective interpretations of Kant. Metz maintains an emphasis on the Kant of practical reason in the context of a political theology. He also accurately situates the profound effect of the "transcendental Kant" upon the post-Hegelian traditions of phenomenology, existentialism and personalism which, as we have seen, inform Ricoeur's project:

> I am bound to point out in this context that it was the transcendental Kant whose thought was considered by the new theologians working before and after the Second World War, not the Kant of the philosophy of history or the Kant of practical reason. German idealism was therefore considered by the new theologians along the path of certain clear [Hegelian] traditions, embracing phenomenology, existentialism and personalism, to such an extent that present-day systematic theology and apologetics still seem to be determined by the philosophical forms with the tradition of German idealism, even when the latter is not explicitly taken into account.[33]
> ...The constant point of departure for [my early] political theology was that the change to the primacy of praxis in philosophy (Kant, the Enlightenment—Marx) should be regarded as the real Copernican revolution in philosophy and that it was therefore very important not only to solve the basic problem of theological reason as it were this side of idealism, but also to try to do theology on the other side of idealism... [Now] it is theologically important that moral praxis not be socially neutral and politically innocent.[34]

I am still compelled to ask of Ricoeur which Kant he follows, "the transcendental Kant" or "the Kant of practical reason"? (Ricoeur himself uses this distinction.) When it comes to the activity of the mythico-poetic imagination Ricoeur seems to oscillate between two different Kants. In the end, this remains a problem. According to Ricoeur, the primary responsibility which accompanies the mythico-poetic imagination is to recognize the nature of the worlds opened up by authors and text.[35] He claims that reflective judgment, in Kantian terms, is to discern the critical difference between mythical texts that mystify and those that give an authentic unity to the life of an individual as part of a community. Yet is

---

[33] Metz, *Faith in History and Society*, p. 23.
[34] Ibid., p. 53–54.
[35] Ricoeur, *Narrative and Time*, III, pp. 246–49.

such judgment sufficient to ensure the truth and justice of the forms of praxis constituted by the mythico-poetic imagination? I want to stress that praxis is never socially neutral nor politically innocent.

I must, therefore, conclude that, in the face of possibly undermining questions concerning truth and illusion, Ricoeur's fundamental orientation remains that of a positive hermeneutics of faith. But this means that to develop a more penetrating, radical hermeneutics of suspicion he would have to question his own transcendental idealist presuppositions and, in particular, the mysterious functioning of the mythico-poetic imagination.[36] Far from taking Ricoeur's own hermeneutics of suspicion for granted, my opinion is that his hermeneutics needs, if it is to be critically restored, to be radicalized. If he is to be true to his twofold hermeneutic task, authentic faith demands a continual critical reconstruction of the very narratives which structure not only liberating memory but the practical and symbolic dimensions of human willing. Ricoeur has in part offered the possibility of this dual hermeneutical process in *Time and Narrative* I–III by taking seriously the need for history to present criticism of *mythos*, i.e. narrative configuration which points to an omnitemporality.

My position is to assert that the subject matter of both contemporary philosophy and theology must be understood as inherently historical. In keeping with Ricoeur's now well-known conflict of interpretations approach to opposed and contestable standpoints, this position is no doubt contentious. His critical and restorative hermeneutics supports a claim that concepts such as free will, original innocence, and kingdom of God should be understood in the light of both their primordial origin and their future goal. This view could, however, be disputed from his Kantian standpoint since, according to this, the irrevocable *arche* and the unrealizable *telos* of human history are limiting concepts which cannot be known in themselves. In fact Ricoeur's hermeneutics of suspicion and his

---

[36] Some scholars might argue that, by confronting both Descartes and Nietzsche as figures of "the cogito" and "the anticogito", respectively, Ricoeur has developed a more penetrating self-critique in the first chapter of *Soi-même comme un autre*. However, I am not persuaded that Ricoeur develops here a radical hermeneutics which confronts his own transcendental idealism. In fact, it seems just the opposite is the case: *Soi-même comme un autre* confirms his post-Kantian, transcendental idealist position as has been outlined in the preceding chapters of this book. See my "Agnosticism and Attestation: An Aporia concerning the Other in *Oneself as Another*," paper given at "Thinking to 2000," Sixth Conference on Literature and Religion, University of Glasgow, 25 September 1992 (publication, forthcoming).

more recent emphasis on history as determining the conditions for the mythico-poetic imagination offer a possible critique of his own poetics of human willing.

Ricoeur's poetics is equally constituted by and constitutes a projected telos. This is so precisely because, in terms approaching the postmodernist idea of deferral, its historical horizon can always only be in the future and so is necessarily both incomplete and unknowable from the standpoint of the present.[37] What, then, in the light of this consciousness of history can be said ultimately about Ricoeur's restoration of the myths concerning the end of evil? Is there an omnitemporality, an eternity represented by mythical consciousness which is dialectically related to historical consciousness? If so, does this contradict the non-closure of history? Ricoeur, of course, is tempted by a Hegelian totalization of history in eternity.

To address this problem concerning history and the horizon represented by the mythico-poetic imagination, it seems appropriate once more to quote the literary critic Geoffrey Hartman. Hartman describes the tension between history and a transsignifying vision as follows:

> With so much historical knowledge, how can we avoid historicism, or the staging of history as a drama in which epiphanic raptures are replaced by epistemic ruptures, *coupures* as decisive as Hellene and Hebrew, or Hegel and Marx. Can a history be written that does not turn into something monumental and preemptive? In *The Unmediated Vision* I described Romantic and post-Romantic poets in their struggle against mediatedness, in their desire for the kind of vision denounced by Althusser and deconstructed by Derrida, but I was unable to formulate a theory of reading that would be historical rather than historicist.[38]

Admittedly, for Ricoeur, historical consciousness determines the limitations on any unmediated poetic vision. Yet the unfinished horizon of historical consciousness also constitutes the transformative and

---

[37] In "Mapping the Postmodern," Andrea Huyssen claims, "The point is not to eliminate the productive tension between... history and text, between engagement and the mission of art. The point is to heighten that tension, even to rediscover it and to bring it back into focus in the arts as well as in criticism. No matter how troubling it may be, the landscape of the postmodern surrounds us. It simultaneously delimits and opens our horizons. It's our problem and our hope." [Linda J. Nicholson (ed.), *Feminism/Postmodernism* (London: Routledge, 1990), p. 271]

[38] Geoffrey Hartman, *Saving the Text: Literature/Derrida/ Philosophy* (Baltimore: The Johns Hopkins University Press, 1981), p. xx.

transsignifying possibilities of human praxis in opening up new worlds. In turn, these possibilities serve in the critical restoration and ontological reconstitution of the human bond with the sacred.[39] Here Hartman's point can be made as well: this vision would be denounced by the Marxist structuralist Louis Althusser and the poststructuralist Jacques Derrida—two of Ricoeur's French contemporaries.

Notwithstanding such critics, Ricoeur affirms certain tensions:[40]

> Our expectations must be determined, hence finite and relatively modest, if they are to be able to give rise to responsible commitments. We have to keep our horizon of expectation from running away from us. We have to connect it to the present by means of a series of intermediary projects that we may act upon. ... Like Kant, I hold that every expectation must be a hope for humanity as a whole, that humanity is not one species except insofar as it has one history, and, reciprocally, that for there to be such a history, humanity as a whole must be its subject as a collective singular.[41]
>
> ...[however] it is in the mode of lamentation, within the horizon of...eternity, that the Augustinian soul finds itself exiled to the "region of dissimilarity." The moanings of the lacerated soul are indivisibly those of...the sinner. In this way, Christian consciousness takes into account the great elegy that crosses cultural frontiers and sings in a minor key about the sorrow of the finite. ...[yet] it is with a note of hope that the Augustinian soul traverses levels of temporalization that are always less "distended" and more "firmly held," bearing witness that eternity can affect the interior of temporal experience, hierarchizing it into levels, and thereby deepening it rather than abolishing it.[42]

Again we see the ways in which Ricoeur's reconstructions of Kant and Augustine inform his inevitably idealist conception of the tensions between the finitude of historical consciousness and the transsignifying vision expressed poetically in the lamentations of the sinner.

---

[39] Ricoeur, *Fallible Man*, p. 7ff.

[40] Roland Barthes sees this very same tension as the dilemma between ideology and poetry: "(that is) either to posit a reality which is entirely permeable to history, and ideologize; or, conversely, to posit a reality which is *ultimately* impenetrable, irreducible, and in this case, poeticize. In a word, I do not yet see a synthesis between ideology and poetry (by poetry I understand, in a very general way, the search for the inalienable meaning of things)." [Barthes, "Myth Today," in *Mythologies*, trans. Annette Lavers, (London: Jonathan Cape, 1972), pp. 158–59] Also see Bernard Stevens, "*Action et narrativité chez Paul Ricoeur et Hannah Arendt,*" *Etudes phénoménologiques*, tome 1, no. 2 (1985), especially pp. 94–98.

[41] Ricoeur, *Narrative and Time*, III, p. 215.

[42] Ibid., pp. 264–65.

We have found that Ricoeur's philosophy of the will gives meaning to ancient myths concerning the origin of evil insofar as these may be critically restored by way of recognizing human temporality/non-temporality, fallibility, and captivity. Such recognition points to the loss of a bond with the sacred. Ricoeur's project has also provided us with the ontological and conceptual framework for grasping the redemptive tasks of contemporary thought. Yet these essentially transformative and transsignifying tasks remain unrealized: they would have as their constant aim the deliverance of experience in and through both history and society.

Bibliography

Albano, Peter (1976), *Freedom, Truth and Hope: The Relation of Philosophy and Religion in the Thought of Paul Ricoeur*, PhD Dissertation (Claremont University); (Landam, MD: University Press of America, 1986).

Alexander, Ian (1970), "Maine de Biran and Phenomenology," *Journal of the British Society for Phenomenology*, vol. I, pp. 24–35.

Allen, Louis (1970), "Son of Calepin: The French Scene," *New Blackfriars*, vol. 51, no. 605 (October), pp. 479–89.

Allison, Henry E. (1987), "Transcendental Idealism: The 'Two Aspect' View," in Bernard den Ouden and Marcia Moen (eds), *New Essays on Kant* (New York/Bern: Peter Lang), pp. 155–78.

Allison, Henry E. (1990), *Kant's Theory of Freedom* (Cambridge: Cambridge University Press).

Alter, Robert and Kermode, Frank (eds) (1987), *The Literary Guide to the Bible* (London: Collins).

Althusser, Louis (1971), *Lenin and Philosophy and Other Essays*, trans. Ben Brewster (London: New Left Review).

Anderson, Pamela (1991), "Paul Ricoeur's Aesthetics: Tradition and Innovation," *Bulletin de la société americaine de philosophie de langue française*, vol. III, no. 3 (special issue on Paul Ricoeur, edited David Stewart), pp. 207–220.

Anderson, Pamela (1992), "A Question of Personal Identity," *The Personalist Forum*, vol. VIII, no. 1 (spring), pp. 55–68.

Anderson, Pamela (1992), "Ricoeur and Hick on Evil: Post-Kantian Myth?" *Contemporary Philosophy*, vol. XIV, no. 6, pp. 15–20.

Anderson, Pamela (1993), "Narrative Identity and the Mythico-Poetic Imagination," in David Klemm and William Schweiker (eds), *Meanings in Texts and Actions: Questioning Paul Ricoeur* (Charlottesville: University Press of Virginia), pp. 195–204.

Arbib, Michael and Hesse, Mary (1986), *The Construction of Reality* (Cambridge: University Cambridge Press).

Armstrong, A. H. (1972), "St Augustine and Christian Platonism," in R. A. Markus (ed.), *Augustine: A Collection of Critical Essays* (Garden City, NY: Doubleday), pp. 3–37.

Augustine (1961), *The Confessions*, trans. with an Introduction by R.S. Pine-Coffin (Harmondsworth: Penguin Books).

Bachelard, Gaston (1969), *The Poetics of Space*, trans. Maria Jolas (Boston: Beacon Press).

Barth, Karl (1956), "Christ and Adam: Man and Humanity in *Romans* 5," trans. T. A. Smail, *Scottish Journal of Theology*, Occasional Paper No. 5.

Barth, Karl (1960), *Church Dogmatics*, vol. III, no. 2 "Doctrine of Creation," trans. G. W. Bromiley and R. J. Ehrlich (Edinburgh: T and T Clark).

Barthes, Roland (1972), *Mythologies*, trans. Annette Lavers (London: Jonathan Cape).

Baynes, Kenneth, Bohman, James and McCarthy, Thomas (eds) (1987), *After Philosophy: End or Transformation* (Cambridge, MA: MIT Press).

Beck, Lewis (1960), *A Commentary on Kant's Critique of Practical Reason* (Chicago: University of Chicago Press).

Benjamin, Walter (1973), "Theses on the Philosophy of History," in Hannah Arendt (ed.), *Illuminations*, trans. Harry Zohn (London: Fontana Collins), pp. 255–66.

Bennett, Jonathan (1966), *Kant's Analytic* (Cambridge: Cambridge University Press).

Bennett, Jonathan (1974), *Kant's Dialectic* (Cambridge: Cambridge University Press).

Bernstein, J. M. (1987), "A Poetics of the Will," *The Times Higher Education Supplement* (27 March), p. 19.

Bernstein, Richard (1972), *Praxis and Action* (London: Duckworth).

Bourgeois, P. L. (1975), *Extension of Ricoeur's Hermeneutic* (The Hague: Martinus Nijhoff).

Brown, David (1987), *Continental Philosophy and Modern Theology* (Oxford: Basil Blackwell).

Bullock, Alan and Woodings, R. B. (eds) (1983), *The Fontana Biographical Companion to Modern Thought* (London: Fontana Collins).

Butler, Judith (1987), *Subjects of Desire: Hegelian Reflections in Twentieth-Century France* (New York: Columbia University Press).

Carnois, Bernard (1987), *The Coherence of Kant's Doctrine of Freedom*, trans. David Booth (Chicago: University of Chicago Press).

Carr, David (1986), *Time, Narrative and History* (Bloomington: Indiana University Press).

Clark, S. H. (1990), *Paul Ricoeur* (London: Routledge).

Cullmann, Oscar (1951), *Christ and Time: The Primitive Christian Conception of Time and History*, trans. Floyd V. Filson (London: SCM Press).

Dallmayr, Fred R. (1987), *Critical Encounters: Between Philosophy and Politics* (Notre Dame: University of Notre Dame Press).

Daly, Mary (1986), *Beyond God the Father: Toward a Philosophy of Women's Liberation* (London: The Women's Press).

Dauenhauer, Bernard P. (ed.) (1987), *At The Nexus of Philosophy and History* (Athens: The University of Georgia Press).

De Beauvoir, Simone (1965), *Force of Circumstance*, trans. Richard Howard (New York: Putnam).

De Man, Paul (1983), *Blindnesss and Insight: Essays in the Rhetoric of Contemporary Criticism* (London: Methuen).

Deleuze, Gilles (1983), *Nietzsche and Philosophy*, trans. Hugh Tomlinson (London: Athlone).

Deleuze, Gilles and Guattari, Felix (1987), *A Thousand Plateaus*, trans. Brian Massumi (London: Athlone).

Derrida, Jacques (1973), *Speech and Phenomena*, trans. David B. Allison (Evanston: Northwestern University Press).

Descombes, Vincent (1980), *Modern French Philosophy*, trans. Linda Scott-Fox and J. M. Harding (Cambridge: Cambridge University Press).

Dews, Peter (1987), *Logics of Disintegration: Post-Structuralist Thought and The Claims of Critical Theory* (London: Verso).

Donoghue, Denis (1981), *Ferocious Alphabets* (London: Faber & Faber).

Dornisch, Loretta (1973), *A Theological Interpretation of the Meaning of Symbol in the Theory of Paul Ricoeur and Possible Implications for Contemporary Education*, PhD Dissertation (Marquette University).

Esprit: Changer la culture et la politique (1988), tomes 7–8, no. 140–41 *(juillet-août)*.

Field-Bibb, Jacqueline (1989), "'By Any Other Name': The Issue of Inclusive Language," *The Modern Churchman*, vol. XXXI, no. 2: 5–9.

Field-Bibb, Jacqueline (1991), *Women Towards the Priesthood: Ministerial Politics and Feminist Praxis* (Cambridge: Cambridge University Press).

Flores, Ralph (1984), *The Rhetoric of Doubtful Authority* (Ithaca: Cornell University Press).

Foucault, Michel (1970), *The Order of Things: An Archaelogy of the Human Sciences*, trans. Alan Sheridan Smith (London: Tavistock).

Gadamer, Hans-Georg (1981), *Reason in the Age of Science*, trans. Frederick G. Lawrence (Cambridge, MA: MIT Press).

Gerhart, Mary (1979), *The Question of Belief In Literary Criticism: An Introduction to the Hermeneutical Theory of Paul Ricoeur* (Stuttgart: Akademischer Verlag Hans-Dieter Heinz).

Gerhart, Mary (1984), "Paul Ricoeur," in Dean G. Peerman and Martin E. Marty (eds), *A Handbook of Christian Theologians* (Nashville: Abingdon Press), pp. 608–24.

Girard, René (1977), *Violence and the Sacred*, trans. Patrick Gregory (Baltimore: The Johns Hopkins University Press).

Girard, René (1987), *Things Hidden Since the Foundation of the World*, research in collaboration with Jean Michel Ougho and Guy Lefort, trans. Stephen Bann (Books II and III) and Michael Metteer (Book I) (London: Athlone).

Guyer, Paul (ed.) (1992), *The Cambridge Companion to Kant* (Cambridge: Cambridge University Press).

Habermas, Jürgen (1972), "Walter Benjamin: Consciousness-Raising or Rescuing Critique," in Gary Smith (ed.) (1988), *On Walter Benjamin: Critical Essays and Recollections* (Cambridge, MA: MIT Press), pp. 90–128.

Habermas, Jürgen (1979), *Communication and the Evolution of Society*, trans. Thomas McCarthy (Boston: Beacon Press).

Habermas, Jürgen (1983), *The Theory of Communicative Action*, vol. I *Reason and the Rationalisation of Society*, trans. Thomas McCarthy (London: Heineman).

Habermas, Jürgen (1987), *The Theory of Communicative Action*, vol. II *Lifeworld and System: A Critique of Functionalist Reason*, trans. Thomas McCarthy (Cambridge: Polity Press in association with Basil Blackwell).

Habermas, Jürgen (1988), *The Philosophical Discourse of Modernity*, trans. Frederick Lawrence (Cambridge: Polity Press in association with Basil Blackwell).

Hart, R. L. (1968), *Unfinished Man and the Imagination: Toward an Ontology and a Rhetoric of Revelation* (New York: Herder and Herder).

Hartman, Geoffrey H. (1980), *Criticism in the Wilderness: The Study of Literature Today* (New Haven: Yale University Press).

Hartman, Geoffrey H. (1981), *Saving the Text: Literature /Derrida/Philosophy* (Baltimore: The Johns Hopkins University Press).

Hegel, G. W. F. (1975), *Lectures on the Philosophy of World History: Introduction - Reason in History*, trans. Duncan Forbes (Cambridge: Cambridge University Press).

Hegel, G. W. F. (1977), *Phenomenology of Spirit*, trans. A.V. Miller (Oxford: Clarendon Press).

Heidegger, Martin (1967), *Being and Time*, trans. John Macquarrie and Edward Robinson (Oxford: Basil Blackwell).

Heller, Agnes (1987), *Beyond Justice* (Oxford: Basil Blackwell).

Hick, John (1968), *Evil and the God of Love* (London: Collins Fontana).

Hick, John (1969), Book Review, *Theology Today*, vol. 24, no. 4, pp. 521–522.

Hillis Miller, J. (1987), *The Ethics of Reading* (New York: Columbia University Press).

Hillis Miller, J. (1987), "But Are Things As We Think They Are?" *The Times Literary Supplement* (9 October), pp. 1104–1105.

Hodgson, P.C. and King, R.H. (eds) (1985), *Readings in Christian Theology* (Philadelphia: Fortress Press).

Hooker, Morna (1967), *The Son of Man in Mark: A Study of the Background of the term "Son of Man" and its use in St Mark's Gospel* (London: SPCK).

Husserl, Edmund (1950), *Idées directrices pour une phénoménologie, Tome premier: Introduction générale à la phénoménologie*, trad. de Paul Ricoeur (Paris: Editions Gallimard).

Husserl, Edmund (1964), *The Phenomenology of Internal Time-Consciousness*, trans. J. S. Churchill (Bloomington: Indiana University Press).

Husserl, Edmund (1973), *Cartesian Meditations*, trans. Dorion Cairns (The Hague: Martinus Nijhoff).

Husserl, Edmund (1977), *La Crise de l'humanité européenne et la philosophie*, trad. de Paul Ricoeur, Préface du Dr S. Strasser (Paris: Aubier Montaigne).

Husserl, Edmund (1981), *Husserl: Shorter Works*, edited by Peter McCormick and Frederick A. Elliston with a Foreword by Walter Biemel (Notre Dame, IN: University of Notre Dame Press/ Brighton, Sussex: The Harvester Press).

Hyppolite, Jean (1974), *Genesis and Structure of Hegel's Phenomenology of Spirit*, trans. Samuel Cherniak and John Heckman (Evanston: Northwestern University Press).

Ihde, Don (1971), *Hermeneutic Phenomenology: The Philosophy of Paul Ricoeur* (Evanston: Northwestern University Press).

Jameson, Fredric (1981), *The Political Unconscious: Narrative as a Socially Symbolic Act* (London: Methuen).

Jasper, David (1987), "The Limits of Formalism and The Theology of Hope: Ricoeur, Moltmann and Dostoyevsky," *Literature and Theology*, vol. 1, no. 1 (March), pp. 1–10.

Jaspers, Karl (1952), *"Le mal radical chez Kant,"* *Deucalion*, vol. 4, no. 36, pp. 227–52.

Jaspers, Karl (1967), *Philosophical Faith and Revelation*, trans. E. B. Ashton (London: Collins).

Jaspers, Karl (1969/70), *Philosophy*, 3 vols, trans. E. B. Ashton (Chicago: University of Chicago Press).

Jaspers, Karl (1981), "Reply to My Critics," in Paul Arthur Schilpp (ed.), *The Philosophy of Karl Jaspers*, second, augmented edition (LaSalle: Open Court Publishing Co.), pp. 748–869.

Jeanrond, Werner G (1988), "Hermeneutics and Christian Praxis: Some Reflections on the History of Hermeneutics," *Literature and Theology*, vol. 2, no. 2 (September), pp. 174–88.

Jefferson, Anne and Robey, David (eds) (1986), *Modern Literary Theory: A Comparative Introduction*, second edn (London: B. T. Batsford).

Kant, Immanuel (1950), *Critique of Pure Reason*, trans. Norman Kemp Smith (London: Macmillan).

Kant, Immanuel (1951), *The Moral Law: The Groundwork of the Metaphysics of Morals*, trans. John Paton (London: Hutchinson).

Kant, Immanuel (1956), *Critique of Practical Reason*, trans. Lewis White Beck (Indianapolis: Bobbs-Merrill).

Kant, Immanuel (1960), *Religion within the Limits of Reason Alone*, trans. Theodore Greene and Hoyt Hudson (New York: Harper and Row).

Kant, Immanuel (1964), *The Doctrine of Virtue*, trans. Mary Gregor (New York: Harper and Row).

Kant, Immanuel (1985), *On History*, trans. Lewis White Beck, Robert E. Anchor and Emil L. Fackenheim (New York: Macmillan).

Kearney, Richard (1984), *Poétique du possible: Phénoménologie herméneutique de la figuration* (Paris: Beauchesne).

Kearney, Richard (1984), *Dialogues with Contemporary Continental Thinkers: The Phenomenological Heritage* (Manchester: Manchester University Press).

Kearney, Richard (1987), *Modern Movements in European Philosophy* (Manchester: Manchester University Press).

Kearney, Richard (1988), *The Wake of Imagination: Ideas of Creativity in Western Culture* (London: Hutchinson).

Kemp, T. Peter and Rasmussen, David (eds) (1989), *The Narrative Path: The Later Works of Paul Ricoeur* (Cambridge, MA: MIT Press).

Klemm, David E. (1983), *The Hermeneutical Theory of Paul Ricoeur: A Constructive Analysis* (London/Toronto: Associated University Press).

Klemm, David E. (1987), "Toward a Rhetoric of Post-Modern Theology: Through Barth and Heidegger," *Journal of the American Academy of Religion*, vol. LV, no. 3 (fall), pp. 443–72.

Klemm, David E. (1989), "Ricoeur, Theology and the Rhetoric of Overturning," *Literature and Theology* vol. 3, no. 3 (November), pp. 267–84.

Kojève, Alexandre (1969), *Introduction to the Reading of Hegel*, trans. J.H. Nichols (New York: Basic Books).

Kristeva, Julia (1982), *Powers of Horror: An Essay on Abjection*, trans. Leon S. Roudiez (New York: Columbia University Press).

Lacoue-Labarthe, Philippe (1990), *Heidegger, Art and Politics*, trans. Chris Turner (Oxford: Basil Blackwell).

Levi-Strauss, Claude (1966), *The Savage Mind* (Chicago: University of Chicago Press).

Lewis, J.J. (1991), "Synthesis and Category: Synthesis of the Heterogeneous Ricoeur and Kant," *Bulletin de la société americaine de philosophie de langue française*, special issue on Paul Ricoeur, edited David Stewart, vol. III, no. 3, pp. 183–206.

Lindars, Barnabas (1983), *Jesus Son of Man: A Fresh Examination of the Son of Man Sayings in the Gospels in Light of Recent Research* (London: SPCK).

Lobkowicz, Nicholas (1967), *Theory and Practice: History of a Concept from Aristotle to Marx* (Notre Dame: University of Notre Dame Press).

Lowe, W. J. (1977), *Mystery of the Unconscious: A Study in the Thought of Paul Ricoeur* (New Jersey: The Scarecrow Press; The American Theological Library Association).

Lyotard, Jean-François (1984), *The Postmodern Condition: A Report on Knowledge*, trans. Geoff Bennington and Brian Massumi (Minneapolis: University of Minnesota Press).

Lyotard, Jean-François (1988), *The differend: phrases in dispute*, trans. George Van Den Abbeele (Minneapolis: University of Minnesota Press).

MacLean, Ian (1986), "Reading and Interpretation: Ricoeur," in Anne Jefferson and David Robey (eds), *Modern Literary Theory: A Comparative Introduction*, second edn (London: B. T. Batsford), pp. 136–38.

Macquarrie, John (1973), *Existentialism* (Harmondsworth: Penguin Books).

Marcel, Gabriel (1935), *Etre et avoir* (Paris: Aubier, Coll. *"Philosophie de l'Esprit"*); trans. K. Farrer, *Being and Having* (New York: Harper, 1965).

Marcel, Gabriel (1940), *Du Refus à l'invocation* (Paris: Gallimard, Coll. *"Esprit"*).

Markus, R. A. (ed.) (1972), *Augustine: A Collection of Critical Essays* (Garden City, NY: Doubleday).

Marx, Karl and Engels, Friedrich (1976), *Collected Works*, vol. 5 (London: Lawrence and Wishart).

McCarthy, Thomas (1991), *Ideals and Illusions: On Reconstruction and Deconstruction in Contemporary Critical Theory* (Cambridge, MA: MIT Press).

McFague, Sallie (1982/3), *Metaphorical Theology: Models of God in Religious Language* (Philadelphia: Fortress/London: SCM Press).

McLellan, David (1969), *The Young Hegelians and Karl Marx* (London: Macmillan).

Merleau-Ponty, Maurice (1962), *The Phenomenology of Perception*, trans. Colin Smith (London: Routledge and Kegan Paul).

Metz, Johann Baptist (1980), *Faith in History and Society*, trans. David Smith (Tunbridge Wells, Kent: Burns and Oats).

Moltmann, Jürgen (1967), *Theology of Hope: On the Grounds and Implications of a Christian Eschatology*, trans. James W. Leitch (London: SCM Press).

Moltmann, Jürgen (1974), *The Crucified God: The Cross of Christ as the Foundation and Criticism of Christian Theology*, trans. R.A. Wilson and John Bowden (London: SCM Press).

Moltmann-Wendel, Elisabeth and Moltmann, Jürgen (1984), *Humanity in God* (London: SCM Press).

Montefiore, Alan (ed.) (1983), *Philosophy in France Today* (Cambridge: Cambridge University Press).

Montefiore, Alan (1986), "In and Out of Time," *The Times Literary Supplement* 17 January, p. 68.

Mudge, Lewis (1980), "Paul Ricoeur on Biblical Interpretation," in *Essays on Biblical Interpretation* (Philadelphia: Fortress Press), pp. 1–40.

Nabert, Jean (1943), *Eléments pour une éthique* (Paris: Aubier); (1969) *Elements for an Ethic*, trans. William J. Petrek with a Preface by Paul Ricoeur (Evanston: Northwestern University Press).

Nabert, Jean (1955), *Essai sur la mal* (Paris: Presses Universitaire de France).

Nabert, Jean (1966), *Le désir de Dieu*, Préface de Paul Ricoeur (Paris: Aubier-Montaigne).

Nietzsche, Friedrich (1956), *The Birth of Tragedy and The Genealogy of Morals*, trans. Francis Golffing (Garden City, NY: Doubleday).

Norris, Christopher (1991), *Deconstruction: Theory and Practice*, rev edn (London: Routledge).

O'Malley, John (1972), *Sociology of Meaning* (London: Human Context Books).

O'Neill, Onora (1986), "The Power of Example," *Philosophy*, vol. 61, pp. 7–29.

O'Neill, Onora (1987), Book Review, *Bulletin of the Hegel Society of Great Britain*, no. 15, pp. 38–44.

O'Neill, Onora (1989), *Constructions of Reason: Explorations of Kant's Practical Philosophy* (Cambridge: Cambridge University Press).

O'Neill, Onora (1991), Book Review, *Bulletin of the Hegel Society of Great Britain*, nos 23/24, pp. 108–11.

O'Neill, Onora (1992), "Vindicating Reason," in Paul Guyer (ed.), *The Cambridge Companion to Kant* (Cambridge: Cambridge University Press), pp. 280–308.

Passmore, John (1985), *Recent Philosophers: A Supplement to A Hundred Years of Philosophy* (London: Duckworth).

Paton, H.J. (1971), *The Categorical Imperative: A Study in Kant's Moral Philosophy* (Philadelphia: University of Pennsylvania Press).

Placher, William (1987), "Paul Ricoeur and Postliberal Theology: A Conflict of Interpretations?" *Modern Theology*, vol. 4, no. 1 (October), pp. 35–52.

Peukert, Helmut (1984), *Science, Action and Fundamental Theology: Toward a Theology of Communicative Action*, trans. James Bohman (Cambridge, MA: MIT Press).

Pippin, Robert B. (1990), *Modernism as a Philosophical Problem* (Oxford: Basil Blackwell).

Prendergast, Christopher (1986), *The Order of Mimesis: Balzac, Stendahl, Nerval, Flaubert* (Cambridge: Cambridge University Press).

Rasmussen, David (1971), *Mythic-Symbolic Language and Philosophical Anthropology: A Constructive Interpretation of the Thought of Paul Ricoeur* (The Hague: Martinus Nijhoff).

Reardon, Bernard (1988), *Kant as Philosophical Theologian* (London: Macmillan).

Redding, Paul (1991), "Hermeneutic or Metaphyiscal Hegelianism: Kojève's Dilemma," *The Owl of Minerva: Biannual Journal of the Hegel Society of America*, vol. 22, no. 2 (spring), pp. 175–89.

Ricoeur, Paul (1947), *Gabriel Marcel et Karl Jaspers: Philosophie du mystère et philosophie du paradoxe* (Paris: Temps Présent).

Ricoeur, Paul (1957), "*La philosophie politique d'Eric Weil*," *Esprit*, 25, no. 10 (octobre), pp. 412–28.

Ricoeur, Paul (1957), "The Relation of Jaspers' Philosophy to Religion," in Paul Arthur Schilpp (ed.), *The Philosophy of Karl Jaspers: A Critical Analysis and Evaluation*, (New York: Tudor), pp. 611–42; second augmented edition 1981, Schilpp (ed.) (LaSalle, IL: Open Court Publishing Company), pp. 611–42.

Ricoeur, Paul (1965), *Fallible Man*, trans. Charles Kelbley (Chicago: Henry Regnery); revised Kelbley 1986 with an Introduction by Walter J. Lowe (New York: Fordham University Press). Original French edition (1960, reprinted 1988) *Philosophie de la volonté. Finitude et culpabilité I. L'homme faillible* (Paris: Aubier, Éditions Montaigne).

Ricoeur, Paul (1965), *History and Truth*, trans. Charles Kelbley, second edn (Evanston: Northwestern University Press).

Ricoeur, Paul (1966), *Freedom and Nature: The Voluntary and the Involuntary*, trans. Erazim Kohak (Evanston: Northwestern University Press). Original French edition (1950, reprinted 1988), *Philosophie de la volonté. Le volontaire et l'involontaire* (Paris: Aubier, Éditions Montaigne).

Ricoeur, Paul (1967, reprinted 1969), *The Symbolism of Evil*, trans. Emerson Buchanan (New York/London: Harper and Row; paperback - Boston: Beacon Press). Original French edition (1960, reprinted 1988), *Philosophie de la volonté. Finitude et culpabilité II. La symbolique du mal* (Paris: Aubier, Éditions Montaigne).

Ricoeur, Paul (1967), *Husserl: An Analysis of His Phenomenology*, trans. E. G. Ballard and L. E. Embree (Evanston: Northwestern University Press).

Ricoeur, Paul and MacIntyre, Alasdair (1969), *The Religious Significance of Atheism* (New York: Columbia University Press).

Ricoeur, Paul (1970), *Freud and Philosophy: On Interpretation*, trans. Denis Savage (New Haven: Yale University Press).

Ricoeur, Paul (1973), "A Critique of B. F. Skinner's Beyond Freedom and Dignity," *Philosophy Today*, vol. 17, no. 2/4 (summer), pp. 166–75.

Ricoeur, Paul (1974), *The Conflict of Interpretations: Essays in Hermeneutics*, I, trans. several authors, edited Don Ihde (Evanston: Northwestern University Press).

Ricoeur, Paul (1974), *Political and Social Essays*, edited David Stewart and J. Bien (Athens: Ohio University Press).

Ricoeur, Paul (1975), "Biblical Hermeneutics: the Parables of Jesus," *Semeia*, vol. 4, pp. 27–148.

Ricoeur, Paul (1975), "Phenomenology and Hermeneutics," *Nous* 9, p. 85–102.

Ricoeur, Paul (1976), *Interpretation Theory: Discourse and The Surplus Meaning* (Fort Worth: Texas Christian University).

Ricoeur, Paul (1978), *The Philosophy of Paul Ricoeur: An Anthology of His Work*, edited Charles Reagan and David Stewart (Boston: Beacon Press).

Ricoeur, Paul (1978), *The Rule of Metaphor*, trans. Kathleen McLaughlin and John Costello (London: Routledge and Kegan Paul).

Ricoeur, Paul (1979), *Main Trends in Philosophy* (New York/ London: Holmes and Meier).

Ricoeur, Paul (1979), "Naming God," *Union Seminary Quarterly Review*, vol. 34 (summer), pp. 215–27.

Ricoeur, Paul (1979), "The Metaphorical Process as Cognition, Imagination and Feeling," in Shelden Sacks (ed.), *On Metaphor* (Chicago: The University of Chicago Press), pp. 141–57.

Ricoeur, Paul (1980), *Contribution of French Historiography to the Theory of History*, Zaharoff Lecture 1978–79 (Oxford: Clarendon Press).

Ricoeur, Paul (1980), *Essays on Biblical Interpretation*, edited Lewis Mudge (Philadelphia: Fortress Press).

Ricoeur, Paul (1980), "Narrative Time," *Critical Inquiry* vol. 7, no. 1 (autumn), pp. 169–90.

Ricoeur, Paul (1981), *Hermeneutics and the Human Sciences: Essays on Language, Action and Interpretation*, trans. John B. Thompson (Cambridge: Cambridge University Press).

Ricoeur, Paul (1981), "The Bible and the Imagination," in Hans D. Betz (ed.), *The Bible as a Document of the University* (Chico, CA: Scholars Press), pp. 49–75.

Ricoeur, Paul (1984), *Time and Narrative*, I, trans. Kathleen McLaughlin and David Pellauer (Chicago: University of Chicago Press).

Ricoeur, Paul (1985), *Time and Narrative*, II, trans. Kathleen McLaughlin and David Pellauer (Chicago: University of Chicago Press).

Ricoeur, Paul (1985), "Evil: A Challenge to Philosophy and Theology," *Journal of American Academy of Religion*, vol. LII, no. 4 (December), pp. 635–48.

Ricoeur, Paul (1986), *Lectures on Ideology and Utopia* edited George Taylor (New York: Columbia University Press).

Ricoeur, Paul (1987), "Evil," in Mircea Eliade (ed.), *Encyclopedia of Religion*, vol. 5 (New York: Macmillan), pp. 199–208.

Ricoeur, Paul (1987), "Myth and History," in Mircea Eliade (ed.), *Encyclopedia of Religion*, vol. 10, pp. 273–82.

Ricoeur, Paul (1987), "Teleological and Deontological Structures of Action: Aristotle and/or Kant?" in A. Phillips Griffiths (ed.), *Contemporary French Philosophy* (Cambridge: Cambridge University Press) pp. 99–111.

Ricoeur, Paul (1988), *Time and Narrative*, III, trans. Kathleen Blamey and David Pellauer (Chicago: University of Chicago Press).

Ricoeur, Paul (1989), "The Human Being as the Subject Matter of Philosophy," in T. Peter Kemp and David Rasmussen (eds), *The Narrative Path: The Later Works of Paul Ricoeur* (Cambridge, MA: MIT Press), pp. 89–101.

Ricoeur, Paul (1990), "Interpretative Narrative," in Regina Schwartz (ed.), *The Book and the Text: The Bible and Literary Theory* (Oxford: Basil Blackwell), pp. 237–57.

Ricoeur, Paul (1990), *Soi-même comme un autre* (Paris: Editions du Seuil); (1992), *Oneself as Another*, trans. Kathleen Blamey (Chicago: University of Chicago Press.

Ricoeur, Paul (1991), *From Text to Action: Essays in Hermeneutics*, II, trans. Kathleen Blamey and John Thompson (Evanston: Northwestern University Press).

Ricoeur, Paul (1991), *A Ricoeur Reader: Reflection and Imagination*, edited Mario J. Valdes (Hemel Hempstead: Harvester Wheatsheaf Press).

Ricoeur, Paul (forthcoming), "Self as *Ipse*," Oxford Amnesty Lecture 1992 (London/New York: Basic Books).

Rist, John (1972), "Augustine on Free Will and Predestination," in R. A. Markus (ed.), *Augustine: A Collection of Critical Essays* (Garden City, NY: Doubleday), pp. 218–52.

Rosen, Stanley (1987), *Hermeneutics as Politics* (Oxford: Oxford University Press).

Roth, Micheal (1988), *Knowing and History: Appropriations of Hegel in Twentieth-Century France* (Ithaca: Cornell University Press).

Roviello, Anne-Marie (1988), "L'horizon kantien," *Esprit: Changer la culture et la politique*, tomes 7–8, no. 140–41 (juillet-août), pp. 152–62.

Scott, Nathan (1987), "The House of Intellect in an Age of Carnival: Some Hermeneutical Reflections," *Journal of the American Academy of Religion*, vol. LV, no. 1 (spring), pp. 3–19.

Sidgwick, Henry (1888), "The Kantian Conception of Free Will," *Mind* XIII, pp. 405–12; reprinted 1966 in *Methods of Ethics* (London: Macmillan).

Soskice, Janet (1985), *Metaphor and Religious Language* (Oxford: Oxford University Press).

Spiegelberg, Herbert (1965), *The Phenomenological Movement*, II (The Hague: Martinus Nijhoff).

Steiner, George (1975), *After Babel* (Oxford: Oxford University Press).

Stevens Bernard (1985), "*Action et narrativité chez Paul Ricoeur et Hannah Arendt*," *Etudes phénoménologiques*, tome 1, no. 2, pp. 93–110.

Strawson, P. F. (1966), *The Bounds of Sense: An Essay on Kant's Critique of Pure Reason* (London: Methuen).

Sullivan, Robert (1989), *Immanuel Kant's Moral Theory* (Cambridge: Cambridge University Press).

Taylor, Charles (1975), "*Force et sens, les deux dimensions irréductibles d'une science de l'homme*," in Gary B. Madison (ed.), *Sens et existence: En hommage à Paul Ricoeur* (Paris: Éditions du Seuil), pp. 124–37.

Thompson, John B. (1981), *Critical Hermeneutics: A Study in the Thought of Paul Ricoeur and Jürgen Habermas* (Cambridge: Cambridge University Press).

Thompson, John B. (1984), *Studies in the Theory of Ideology* (Cambridge: Polity Press).

Valdés, Mario J. (1987), *Phenomenological Hermeneutics and the Study of Literature* (Toronto: University of Toronto Press), chapter 4 "Ricoeur and Shared Meaning of Interpretation," pp. 56–70.

Valdés, Mario J. (ed.) (1991), *A Ricoeur Reader: Reflection and Imagination* (Hemel Hampstead: Harvester Wheatsheaf).

Van Leeuwen, T. M. (1981), *The Surplus of Meaning: Ontology and Eschatology in the Philosophy of Paul Ricoeur* (Amsterdam: Rodopi).

Vance, Eugene (1986), *Mervelous Signs: Poetics and Sign Theory in the Middle Ages* (Lincoln: University of Nebraska Press).

Vanhoozer, Kevin (1990), *Biblical Narrative in the Philosophy of Paul Ricoeur* (Cambridge: Cambridge University Press).

Vansina, Frans D. (1964), "*Esquisse, orientation et signification de l'enterprise philosophique de Paul Ricoeur (I–II),*" *Revue de métaphysique et de morale* vol. 69, no. 2, pp. 179–88.

Vansina, Frans D. (1985), *Paul Ricoeur: A Primary and Secondary Systematic Bibliography (1935–1984)* (Louvain-la-Neuve: Éditions de l'institut supérieur de philosophie).

Vermes, Geza (1983), *Jesus and the World of Judaism* (London: SCM Press).

Veyne, Paul (1984), *Writing History: Essay on Epistemology*, trans. Mina Moore-Rinvolucri (Manchester: Manchester University Press).

Von Rad, Gerhard (1962), *Old Testament Theology*, 2 vols., trans. D.M.G. Stalker (Edinburgh: Boyd and Oliver).

Webb, Eugene (1988), *Philosophers of Consciousness: Polanyi, Lonergan, Voegelin, Ricoeur, Girard and Kierkegaard* (Seattle: University of Washington Press).

Weil, Eric (1935), *"De l'intérêt que l'on prend à l'histoire,"* Recherches philosophiques 4.

Weil, Eric (1963), *Problèmes kantiens* (Paris: Vrin).

Whiteside, Kerry H (1988), *Merleau-Ponty and the Foundation of an Existential Politics* (New York: Princeton University Press).

Wood, Allen (1970), *Kant's Moral Religion* (Ithaca: Cornell University Press).

Wood, Allen (ed.) (1984), *Self and Nature in Kant's Philosophy* (Ithaca: Cornell University Press).

Wood, David (ed.) (1991), *On Paul Ricoeur: Narrative and Interpretation* (London: Routledge).

Index